Aland

Written by:
Mary Dickinson

Edited, Revised and Cover Design by:
Graham Carmichael

Copyright © 2012 Philip Law, Catherine Law, Christine Law and Andrew Law

All rights reserved.

No part of this book may be reproduced in any form or by any electronic or mechanical means, including storage and retrieval systems, without the express written permission of the owners of this material. The only exception is by a reviewer, who may quote short excerpts in a review.

First published November 2012

HULL LIBRARIES

5 4072 10223770 2

Dedication

For Mary, Mum, Grandma.
A truly creative spirit.
Your memory lives on in all of us.

Chapter 1
'Evacuees'

The train came trundling slowly to a stop, its body like a giant, swaying pupa, its impervious presence dominating the steel rails. A screech filled our ear drums and a steaming sigh escaped from its iron lungs, as its hissing mocked our apprehensive glances. I had never seen a real train and now, I was standing beside one.

The air was filled with the chattering voices of mums and teachers, evacuees and would-be passengers, who hovered around, unsure, hesitant, watching and wavering. Somewhere in the distance, the babble of a loudspeaker echoed across the platform, as the train ground to a halt. Windows slid down and doors were flung open, adding to the din.

I stood there, clasping at the cardboard box housing my gas mask, the string tight across my chest, as I looked on in wonderment at all this activity. Mum was beside me, her hand on my shoulder, and, as I looked into her eyes, she sighed.

"Now, you be a good girl and do as you are told," she said, as she pushed me gently towards a group of other children. They all stood in zombie fashion, some grubby, dishevelled and wide eyed.

"But, Mam," I pleaded.

"You'll be alright. Mrs Brown will look after you." Mum plunged her hand into her shopping bag and pulled out a little felt doll. "Here you are, love."

I gripped at the doll and shouted, "I thought that you were…"

Mum butted in, "I can't leave your dad. You'll be alright love, I've got to go." She bent down, pecked my cheek and dashed away into the crowd.

At that moment, I felt that I would never see her again. I stared after her and shouted earnestly: "Mam! Mam!" but it was no use; she was gone out of my life, forever. Tears welled inside me, I was so afraid. My legs buckled beneath me and I crouched on the heaving platform feeling forgotten, weeping uncontrollably. Suddenly, I heard a voice.

"Look at this little mite!" Two strong hands lifted me up and this stranger, a big, fat-bosomed lady, held me astride on her hip.

"Come on, pet, I'll look after you."

I wiped the back of my hand across my tear-stained face, gasping as my small body stifled my sobs.

"You'll be alright, pet. Crying won't do any good." She glanced at my name tag.

"Mary; what a nice name, your mummy will come and visit you. Meanwhile, you are going to stay on a farm. Won't that be fun?" She looked into my eyes. "You must be the baby here."

I found my voice, indignant though it was, "I'll be five soon."

I now felt a hatred for my mother, which was to fester deep inside me in the years to come. Mrs Brown wiped my red eyes and, as I blew on her handkerchief, I vowed to make the best of my legacy of loneliness.

She sat me on her knee, we had a seat by the window and I held my little felt doll close to my cheek, my body still heaving, as my sobs slowly subsided. I stared around at the other children, some laughing, some crying and a sudden excitement filled my being. I looked up at this kind lady as she patted my knee.

"Better now?" she asked, smiling through pursed lips.

Sobs still controlling my body, I nodded. I remembered that very morning, Dad had kissed me and told me that he loved me very much and that I had to be a brave girl for him - but Mam, well, she left me alone, I would never forgive her for that.

That day on the platform was a stepping stone in my short life. There was a war and I was an angry mixed-up four year old, wanting so much to be grown up. I sat back and rested in the warmth of my new-found friend. Her lap was cosy and my anxious, shaking body slowly relaxed in the nap of her coat sleeve. Tiredness overwhelmed me and sleep soon came.

There was a shrill whistle. My eyelids smarted after so many tears, but I was soon quite alert and, as I stared around me, I felt Mrs Brown's hands tighten as she held me on her lap.

"Have a good sleep, dear?" she asked. I nodded shyly, feeling a little apprehensive.

The carriage was full; next to me sat an old lady, concentrating on her book, but she looked up at me and smiled. I leaned over and saw a boy with a shock of red hair, staring back at me. He had pale blue eyes and a freckled brow. Suddenly, he pulled a gruesome face at me by pulling the skin under his eyes and pushing his fingers up his nostrils, which made me shrink back. 'Boys are horrid,' I thought.

At the opposite window was a pretty lady with fair hair in deep, waves. She was making noises to a playful baby on her knee. As she held up the baby's rattle, she spoke in a foreign language.

Everyone sat quietly, rocking in unison with the momentum. I used my imagination and softly sang to myself the sound of the train: 'Diddle dee, diddle da, diddle dee, diddle da'. It was a hypnotic movement of body and mind, but the whistle pierced the air once more; our carriage jerked, we were slowing down.

"We are nearly there, pet." Mrs Brown cupped her strong hands under my small arms, turned in one movement and sat me where she had been sitting. She winced as she stretched after the traumatic journey, and, as the train slowed down, a sudden jolt made her stumble forward as she reached for our cases and gas masks. I noticed her full arms and elbows and the sweat stains under her arm pits, but to me, this lady was strong, kind and loving. She wasn't like my mum at all. Her hair was grey, wispy, and combed back into a plaited bun. Her face was round, like her body, her eyes as tiny bright beads, her cheeks flushed like coral and her lips, sumptuous, thick, and caring; she was nice.

She helped everyone else, then she gently peeled me off my seat and she held my two hands as I stood beside her. She gave me a big grin and I felt her warm palms grip mine with much feeling. I knew that I was going to like her and almost from that moment, my mum was forgotten. We waited until we could step off the train and once more, her strong hands lifted me onto the platform. The farm was a mile away, so we continued our journey in a coach especially provided for evacuees. We were pushed and pressed together, our bodies struggling like the contents of a can of worms. The sun streamed in through the windows; it was now midday, in warm, sticky April - the year 1940. I pressed my nose against the glass and then I rubbed my hot breath away, revealing a brilliant, blue sky. How could people fight one another? My mind raced with unanswered questions.

"Oh, my doll, I've lost her," and tears came once more.

"Here you are, petal." Mrs Brown retrieved my doll from her shopping bag. I liked the way she spoke, she seemed so sincere and I liked the funny names she called me: 'Pet' and 'Petal'. "There now," she whispered. I gripped my felt doll in my grubby hands and, for one fleeting moment, I thought of Mum.

There was excitement around me, a waking awareness about the farm. I bit my bottom lip and stretched my neck to see further. The smell of the scented hedgerows seeped through the stuffy coach and the driver was whistling a song I was soon to learn: 'Run rabbit, run rabbit, run, run, run'. Even though our bodies ached, there was wonderment in the air as we rolled along. Presently the gears on the old coach groaned and, as we came to a halt, Mrs Brown smiled.

"Here's the farm, Mary, watch your step." She held my hand as I jumped off the running board. The mud underfoot had hardened in the sun and, with my doll hanging from one hand, gas mask from the other, I walked along quietly, my knee socks hugging my ankles, as my shoes scattered the stones along the path. We were all taken to a large room and in it, were rows of small bunk beds. Mrs Brown walked up to the first bed and fluffed up the pillow, "It's a lovely bed and all for you."

"No!" I pouted defiantly, "I don't want to sleep there," and I stood, as if glued to the spot. With one swift motion, she lifted me, gently but firmly, sitting me at the foot of the bed.

"There now, you will be with the other children."

I folded my arms and stared around me; all the other children were laughing and jumping on their beds. My eyes widened.

"But I want to stay with you. Don't go away like my mother, please, please?" She was strict, but no one could resist the pleas of a frightened child.

"Very well," she sighed and she lifted me onto her hip, her eyes sparkling. "Maybe, just for tonight, you can sleep in my room."

Relieved, I drew a shaky breath.

The kitchen was large. On the floor were red shiny tiles, a huge pine table dominated the centre and there was a big tabby cat stretched out along the deep window sill. Her body lay pulling on the hem of the net curtains; she was so still, I thought she was a statue.

"Oh," I gasped. I ran to the sill, but couldn't reach her. Mrs Brown smiled.

"That is Connie, she's about the same age as you," she said, slowly lifting her down. Connie was so fluffy, her hair thick and long. She opened her sleepy yellow eyes and yawned, as if telling us to leave her alone and then she closed them again, unperturbed.

I quickly scrambled onto the rocking chair and Connie sat on my lap, quite contented. She was unaware of my need to cuddle and cajole her and, as I stroked her, I felt the warm vibrancy of her deep purr. Mrs Brown washed her hands and proceeded to take a large jug from the fridge. We each had a glass of fresh milk and, as I sipped the sweet cold drink, I watched her methodically fill and pop the kettle on the giant cream stove, which was called an Aga cooker. Steel and copper pans hung from the rafters above and glistened between an assortment of sweet-smelling herbs. Mrs Brown sat down beside me, put her hands on my shoulders and spoke.

"I know your mum couldn't come, love, but I will look after you. But I want no nonsense. You show me how good you can be and stay with the other children tomorrow. After a night's sleep you will feel much better." It was then that I realised she wasn't going to run away from me like my mum had done.

"What's your name?" I asked brightly.

"Well, everybody calls me Auntie."

"Auntie what?" I persisted.

"Betty, I suppose," she laughed.

"Can I call you Auntie B?"

"Of course you can, my pet." She cupped her fat fingers around my small face and gave my forehead a sticky kiss. It was to be the start of a very happy time for me and all the other children. Auntie B seemed to make me feel special - wanted and most of all, loved. We had a meal of thick wedged bread and strawberry jam and as I ate, I realised just how hungry I was.

Chapter 2
'New Friends'

Each day, I began to unwind and join in with the other children. I was no longer afraid and withdrawn, becoming boisterous, bombastic and beaming with energy instead. One morning, Aunt B took me to the chicken house. As we opened the door, a scurry of feathers filled the air and the sound of broody hens muttered at our presence. I watched as Aunt B pushed her hand under a protesting hen and, as if by magic, she produced an egg. I didn't know it, but an egg in the war was a prize indeed, as families were only allowed one egg per weekly ration. She gently placed them onto a tea cloth in the basket and stressed that great care must be taken so as not to damage their delicate shells and then she turned to me, smiling. "If you are a good girl, I'll let you collect the eggs another day." I felt that it would be a great honour, as she told me that it would be a superior task and important for the war effort. At the time, I wasn't quite sure what she meant. I watched her as she balanced the basket on her hip. I found it so easy to talk to her.

"Is this your farm, Auntie?" I asked, as we walked along the cobbled yard.

"Nay, pet, I'm only a helper, but I am here to look after little ones like you."

"You won't go away will you, 'cause my mum did?" I asked anxiously.

"Oh bless you, love. You and me, we make a good team, don't we?" She gave me that impish, chuckling smile, then lifted her head. "It's going to be a lovely warm day; would you help me with the washing?" I nodded eagerly. I could feel a slight breeze as I peered into the blue sky and thoughtfully followed the fluffy clouds as they glided past. Aunt B started to hang up the washing, but I was too small to reach the line, so she gave me a milking stool to give me height. I put a few pegs in the washing, but I felt sure I must have slowed her down a little. When we had finished, Aunt B rested the basket on her hip and stared at me.

"The other children are playing ball, Mary. Don't you want to play with them?"

"No, I want to stay with you, Auntie." She tilted her head to one side, wearing a bemused expression.

"Don't you like to have friends, Mary?" she asked.

"I've got you!" I answered quickly. "I like staying here with you."

Connie came up to me and rubbed her long hairy body against my bare legs. Aunt B handed me her brush. "You groom her, Mary, she likes that." Connie lay on her back and toyed with the brush handle and we played together.

Back in the kitchen, Aunt B gave me Rich Tea biscuits with my milk. A warm aroma filled the air and the wireless droned with the sound of soft music. Suddenly, a man's voice sounded. It was the news. I listened intently and turned to Aunt B.

"Is there still a war on, Auntie?"

"Bless you, pet, I'm afraid so. Listen." She put her index finger to her lips.

The announcer was stating there had been heavy bombing in an East Yorkshire town. Little did I know at the time, he was talking about my home town of Kingston upon Hull. I looked seriously at Aunt B.

"I wonder if my dad is alright."

"I am sure he will be fine, and your mum, too." I didn't think of Mam, only Dad. I missed his hugs and kisses and his storytelling.

The children with whom I slept were older than me. They would whisper together and play in groups, but I didn't feel left out; I liked being a loner. I was constantly living in a world of my own, of make believe. I would whisper to my little doll, which I had named Betsy, as it reminded me of Aunt B, who I loved very much. I would lie in bed, after Aunt B had tucked me in, and squeeze Betsy's soft felt body tightly as I spoke the words: "I won't leave you, Betsy; I won't leave you." I seemed to have a deep uncertainty in my heart as I caressed her.

The next morning was Sunday. Aunt B took me and some of the other children to church, a short walk from the farm. The church seemed cold and uncomfortable. As it was the first time I had ever been inside a church, I stared around me. Aunt B nudged me saying: "This is the house of God." I thought the windows were colourful and pretty and, above the altar, there was this sad statue of Jesus on the cross. The shuffling hymn books and muffled whispers sounded strange in such a great space and as the sound echoed with each movement, I felt a little scared.

When we were walking home, I asked Aunt B where God slept in his big house. Aunt B laughed and wondered at my train of thought. She sighed as she answered, "God is all around us dear, he can do anything. He created everything, like the creatures great and small, like it says in the hymn."

I tugged on Aunt B's arm and looked thoughtful. "Did he create the war?"

She patted my head gently. "No, pet, human beings started the war."

"Who are we fighting?" I asked, earnestly.

"The enemy is Germany; Britain is at war with Germany! We have been at war for over a year now and that is why you are staying here, away from the towns where there are raids. The bombs are not dropped in the countryside, but in the towns, where there are the factories, railways, docks, and all the built-up areas." She stopped suddenly, giving a deep sigh and clearing her throat. I saw she had tears in her eyes.

"Let's talk about something else," she whispered in a broken voice. She smiled at me. "Well I suppose it affects the children as much as the adults."

I felt that I admired her, she seemed to know everything and I was keen to absorb all her knowledge. Also, she was very patient, answering my endless questions without complaint. When we arrived back at the house, some of the other children were playing tig. I stood and watched them. A girl with short cropped hair skipped beside me.

"What's your name, haven't seen you before?" she asked.

"Mary," I answered timidly.

"I'm Jean. I live in Hull really, but I am here with the others." She pointed to the other children, who were shouting and running about. "Do you want to play? You're little aren't you? How old are you?" She laughed at asking all three questions at once.

"I… I'm five," I lied, standing on my tiptoes, determined to look bigger than I was. She grabbed my hand and we ran to the others.

"This is Mary," she announced.

I looked sheepishly at them as they all stared back at me. They were waiting for me to speak. "I… I've been to church," I blurted out.

"Oh, that's boring," shouted a boy from the back of the group, immediately taking charge. "Let's play Hide and Seek. I'll count to ten, then I'm coming."

Jean pulled on my arm. "I know where to go; he will never find us."

We ran through the farm gate and into a big barn. She pulled me down into some straw; I could smell manure. We crouched there for what seemed ages. Jean was right, he didn't find us. Slowly we emerged, looking somewhat bedraggled. We ran and touched the spot where the boy had started his count. "Block you one, two, three," we chanted. We played on for some time and Jean and I became firm friends.

One day, when I walked into the yard, Jean and the others were skipping. She had a skipping rope with yellow lollypop handles and inside the handles, many ball bearings were housed. I tried to skip, but couldn't seem to co-ordinate the rope with the ground beneath me. The other children all laughed at my efforts. Jean chuckled too, but added kindly "You only need to practise, Mary." When I went back to the kitchen, I was sulking. Aunt B was baking scones, unaware of my mood.

"I don't want to play outside. I can't skip like the others anyway."

I scuffed my toes against the door jamb in annoyance and pouted. Aunt B turned to me.

'They are all older than you. You'll learn in time, pet. Here, wash your hands and you can help me."

My deep frown turned into a smile. Aunt B tied a small apron around my waist and placed some baking tins before me. She showed me how to grease them in preparation for the pastry, then she gave me a tiny lump of spare pastry for me to poke, prod and knead. As she spooned jam into her tartlets, she gave me a few currants to adorn my now little, man-shaped pastry. All the time she would tell me what she was doing and while I was helping, I was learning. I loved that time, the smell of baking, the kettle singing on the hob and Connie's whispering movements as she preened and licked her fur by the warm stove.

After a while, I sat in the big pine rocking chair and just watched Aunt B. She gently lifted out the sweet-smelling scones and tarts, and laid them on a cooling tray. I looked longingly at the tempting cakes, especially my little pastry man.

Aunt B smiled and shook her head, "They are very hot, you can have one later." She then took out a piece of greaseproof paper from the table drawer and twisted it around her fingers to make a cone-shaped bag. Into this she placed a dessert spoon full of currants and she reached out to me.

"Have these for being a good girl." This was the next best thing to sweets. Most food and that included sweets, was rationed. One person's sweet ration was a quarter of a pound per week. Four year olds do like sweets; currants just didn't seem the same.

Friday was my favourite day of the week, because Aunt B would walk with me to the village shop. I would stare longingly at the jars of humbugs, barley sugar sticks and rainbow lollipops, my mouth watering. I used to have a treat, two whole ounces of dolly mixtures and instead of chewing them, I would suck them in my mouth to make them last. When we were walking home from the shop, Aunt B's basket looked very heavy.

"I wish I was grown up, then I could carry your basket, Auntie."

"Aye love, don't wish your life away," she would say. She suddenly stopped.

"Mary, I've got something to tell you. It's a surprise." My eyes widened.

"What?" I gasped.

"It's your birthday next week and your mum is coming to see you." Gosh, was it June already; a child doesn't count the days. Each day was an adventure. My birthday was approaching and this time, I really would be five years old, but I thought about my mum and felt that I didn't want to see her at all and I physically shuddered.

"You will be starting school soon, pet, then who will help me in the kitchen?" she laughed.

I frowned, "I don't want to go to school, I want to stay here with you."

Aunt B put her hands on her hips. "School is great fun, you have games, drawing, crayoning, making things."

"Like baking?" I butted in.

"Well maybe," she laughed. "What would you like for your birthday, Mary?" she asked.

"To see my dad," I replied quickly, without hesitation. Aunt B bit her lip and gave a sigh.

"I don't think you will be able to see your dad as he is rather busy, but I am sure he is thinking about you and your mum is coming to see you, that will be nice, won't it?" She waited for my reply. I wasn't overjoyed. Aunt B was mum to me and I didn't like my mum at all.

"Umm……," I grunted, apprehensively. When I went to bed that night, I gripped Betsy tightly and whispered to her, "I'm nearly five years old, Betsy and I don't want to see my mum and I don't want to go to school. All I want to do is to stay with Aunt B."

As the days passed, for a child with a birthday pending, I wasn't very excited. All I could think about were my feelings towards my mother.

I awoke on June 24th, 1940; the cock was crowing and it was still dark outside. I peered through the small window and I could just make out a white mist hovering over the distant fields. I looked at Betsy. "I wish I was a bird so I could fly over the hills to see my dad. I wonder if there is bombing there now. I want to be five, but I don't want to go to school."

At breakfast, Aunt B lifted me off my feet and she smothered me with a sticky kiss. "Happy Birthday, pet," she cooed. "The postman has been."

I quickly scooped up the haphazard cards on the door mat: a card from my Grandma and Granddad Thompson and from my Grandma and Granddad Emmitt. Even my Aunt Enid and my Uncle Sunny had remembered me with a card. Aunt B gave me her card and on it, was a beautiful picture of a cat, just like Connie. My friend, Jean, leaned across the table.

"Open your big envelope, Mary."

My itchy fingers felt its thickness. I opened it gently and found a 'Chelsea' drawing book and a set of pencils wrapped with a card and a letter, but I frowned as I stared at the joined up writing.

Aunt B took the letter from me and began to read: "Dearest Mary, I hope that you are well and happy on the farm, and many, many happy returns of your birthday. When I was a lad, I loved to draw. I hope that you will have some fun with this drawing book. Your mum and I are safe and well and we hope it will not be long before we see one another. Do have a lovely birthday and be a good girl. Lots of love, your Dad. Kisses."

I seized the letter and stared at Dad's writing. Oh, how I missed him at that moment. On the card was printed: 'To dear Mary, much love from Mam and Dad'. Aunt B was beaming that lovely smile of hers.

"Here is my present for you, hope you like it," and she pushed a newspaper parcel across the table.

"I didn't have any wrapping paper," she sighed.

Feverishly, I tore at the paper. There before me was a pink knitted jacket, a knitted skirt and a bonnet, with a rosette of white baby ribbon.

"Doll's clothes," I gasped.

Aunt B's cheeks flushed. "Do you like them, pet?"

"Oh, oh, thank you, thank you!" My constant gasps of joy said it all, as I ran to Aunt B and pulled on her neck with a big hug. "Betsy will look so fine," I shouted with glee. I ran in the bedroom for Betsy and Jean and I sat crossed legged on the clip rug. As I pulled off Betsy's old faded blue dress, Jean watched, wide-eyed, as I redressed the doll. Aunt B had even made holes for tiny mother of pearl buttons. 'How clever Aunt B is,' I thought.

That afternoon the bus was due from Hull and on it would be my mother.

Chapter 3
'Hatred of my Mother'

I tried to push the thoughts of Mum to the back of my mind. I was feeling so happy and the thought of seeing my mother sent me into bellowing doubt. Aunt B was pressing me to eat my breakfast, but as I ate my porridge, I felt that my moments of joy were overshadowed by my awareness of what was to come. Later that morning, Jean and I went to play in our den, in the barn. As we sat on an old blanket laid on straw, we talked. I was admiring Betsy, when Jean grinned, "I've got something for you," and, excitedly, she pulled out a piece of grey cardboard from under her blanket. She had made me a birthday card. She had drawn in crayon: a house, a little girl skipping along the path and other children around - sort of stick people.

"I made it for you," she said, staring deeply into my eyes, waiting for my opinion. The card was dog eared and bent, but it was the best card I had ever owned and, as I stared at the scribbled words, 'Happy Birthday', I knew I had found a good friend.

"And I've brought some new string for our game, 'Cat's Cradle'." Jean held a loop of string in her fingers and showed me how to play. In both her hands, she twisted and slotted the string from her hands to mine. I was having a wonderful birthday, the weather was warm and sunny and a little part of me wanted to see Mum again. The bus was due to arrive at the village green at 2 pm. Aunt B fussed around me like a bee round a honey pot.

"We must have you looking smart," she whispered. I wore my best pink and white gingham check dress, white ankle socks and a pink ribbon in my fair hair.

As I stood, staring down the road, I remembered the last time I had been there; it was only a few weeks ago. Then, I was feeling so lost and abandoned, but now, I was feeling confident, with a sense of belonging, and I wondered how I could have changed so much in so short a time. I suppose the war was to blame. Aunt B turned and looked towards the church clock as the bell struck twice. I felt very confused; with my head tilted to one side, I held Betsy close to my cheek and stared down the lane. I didn't tell Aunt B, but I felt that I didn't love my mum at all. I remembered the day she had walked away from me; try as I might, I could never forget that overwhelming fear inside my body. A scowl came over my small features and I looked on with deep resentment in my heart. I watched the other children waiting and stuck my index finger in my mouth, wondering how they could love their mums after what they had done. They seemed happy, excited, giggling and whispering, the girls slapping their hands together in play, chanting, as I resolved not even to kiss my mother. I kicked at the gravel beneath my feet, gently tapping dust onto my socks, defiantly destroying their rich whiteness. Aunt B didn't see me as she talked with the others. Then I heard Jean's voice.

"They're coming! I can see the coach in the distance. Look!"

As I strained my eyes, I could see what appeared to be two coaches, one on the road and one underneath. The sun was giving the coach its own reflection on the tarmac surface. As its mass flickered into view, the sound of the children's voices reached a crescendo and suddenly a wave of sickness gripped at my stomach and my head reeled. Betsy fell to the ground and I dropped to my knees.

"Whatever's the matter, pet?"

"I… I feel sick," I mumbled, as my body heaved. The other children stared at me, whispering to each other. I felt Aunt B's warm palm on my forehead. She gently wiped my mouth with her hanky.

"There now, I think you were too excited, weren't you, being your birthday and all? Your mum doesn't want to see you poorly, does she?" She held me close and calmed me. "Take some deep breaths and you'll soon feel better."

I knew that my malady was not caused by excitement, but hatred eating at my heart. Aunt B tutted as she tried to wipe the stains off the front of my dress. But, deep inside my mind, I was pleased that my clothes were dishevelled and dirty. In a way, it showed my hostility towards my mother. It never occurred to me that I could be hurting Aunt B.

The screech of brakes filled the air as the large tyres crunched along the gravel beside us and, for a few seconds, the sweet smell of diesel oil made me swallow hard before the fumes abated. I stepped back behind the others, hesitant, waiting. There was a mass of hysteria as children rushed towards the coach to see their loved ones. I watched as all my friends kissed and cuddled their respective mums, as one by one they alighted from the step; then they stopped. The driver jumped out of his cab, yawning and stretching. He walked along the side of the coach and talked with the conductor. He lifted a packet of Woodbines from his breast pocket, lighting his and his partner's cigarettes. Aunt B's hand gripped mine.

"Oh dear," she exclaimed. Thinking that she had missed my mum, she stared around her. She looked towards the conductor. "Are they all off the coach?"

The conductor sighed a mouthful of smoke as he answered, "That's the lot, love; the bus is empty now."

There was exciting chatter all around me, but my mum was nowhere to be seen. Aunt B looked very bewildered. She wandered towards the other mums. I saw them listening to her, then shaking their heads. She came towards me with sadness in her eyes.

"I am so sorry, Mary, your mum doesn't seem to have come."

I looked at the other children, happy and laughing; I wanted to cry, but there were no tears. "Never mind," I said in a matter-of-fact way and I set off down the country lane with Betsy dangling from my hand, by my side. Aunt B rushed towards me, waiting for my distress to show itself in some form, but I felt calm and undisturbed, as if a great burden had been lifted from my mind. As we walked along, Aunt B was suggesting things for us to do, thinking I was unhappy.

"We will walk to Potter's Meadow, where the cows are. Would you like that Mary?"

I nodded. For once I was very subdued, willing to be led. It was a lovely warm balmy day, lots of flies and bees buzzing around. We stopped by a large farm gate; ahead, Friesian cattle were peacefully grazing, tossing their tails without a care. Locking the gate behind us, we ventured into the field and walked towards them. As we came closer, they reared their heads, their huge watery brown eyes asking why we were there. I stood beside one, its wide nostrils furling hot breath. I felt no fear as I put out my hand, stroking its dusty black and white fur. Its whole body heaved as it mooed at me. Its body felt firm and strong, and I was full of curiosity. I had never touched a real cow before.

"Does this one give milk, Auntie?"

"Most of them do; look at their udders, some are full of milk." As they strutted past me, I noticed their clumsy gait, their udders swaying awkwardly.

"It will be milking time at 5 o'clock, and again in the morning. They are taken to the milking parlour. Would you like to see them, Mary?"

"Oh, yes," I replied impatiently.

As we walked along the grass, within only a few minutes, I had forgotten about my mother's presence, or lack of it. She had promised to come; I would never believe her again. It was nice to walk and have Aunt B all to myself. She showed me lots of wild flowers: Shepherds' Purse, Foxgloves, Cowslips, Forget-Me-Nots, Buttercups and Daisies. The field ahead of us was bright yellow, the buttercups were as tall as my knees, so I stopped and picked some, then I ran on ahead. When I looked behind me, Aunt B was a long way off. I didn't feel ill anymore, in fact I felt elated. It was over, the ordeal of meeting Mum again. I didn't care about her at all. Aunt B flopped down on the grass; she was watching me, her hands shading her eyes from the glare of the sun.

"Here you are, Auntie, all for you," and with my arms outstretched, I offered her the buttercups. "Oh they are beautiful, pet, thank you. Here sit down, I know a trick. Let's see if you like butter." She held a buttercup under my chin. "If the yellow glows under your chin, you like butter."

I did the same to Aunt B; she liked butter too. But truthfully, I don't think I had ever tasted butter. I was only given margarine because of food rationing. We both sat quietly for a few minutes absorbing the soothing sun and I chewed on a blade of grass.

Aunt B smiled. "Shall we make a daisy chain for you and your doll? I'll show you how! Firstly pick some long daisies, they must be long mind". Then she methodically slotted the daisies into each other through holes she made in their stalks, and they gradually made a long chain. She held them around my neck, smiling.

"You look as pretty as a picture. Try and make one for Betsy." I attempted it, but was rather clumsy. The stalks kept breaking, so Auntie finished them for me and put them around Betsy's neck.

"You are clever, Auntie," I whispered, with much feeling.

"Nay, pet, it's just something I learnt when I was a child."

I looked thoughtful; I could never imagine Aunt B ever being a little girl like me. I just felt that she was born a plump, kind, loving lady and would stay that way forever. I felt that for the duration I spent with her. She gained my great admiration and I eagerly learned so much about life's rich pattern, as she patiently answered my unending questions. My own mother used to just shrug her shoulders, before quickly changing the subject, obviously not keen to let me indulge my inquisitive nature.

The warm, scented air made me feel sleepy and, that evening after my tea, I didn't go to see the cows. My legs ached as I crawled into bed early, after quite an eventful day and sleep soon came. However, I awoke in the night to the sound of crying. I gripped Betsy tightly, screwed up my eyes, and listened. I could just make out the figure of Aunt B as she slowly opened the door. I heard her voice, she was whispering to a boy at the other side of the room. I listened to her soothing tones, comforting him. The crying gradually stopped and I watched as Aunt B walked towards the door. As she was about to go through it, she stared around at the other children. I quickly closed my eyes and pretended to be asleep. When I heard the door shut, I opened my eyes once more and whispered to Betsy, "I wonder why that boy cried, he's such a baby. He must miss his mummy." I resented his loving thoughts.

I lay there for some time before sleep came; I thought about my mother and started to wonder why she had not come to see me. Then I felt angry with myself for daring to even think about her.

"Betsy, it's our little secret; I vow never to love my mam again, and I hope this war goes on for ever and ever and ever, and then I can stay with Aunt B." I didn't realise what a self-centred child I was turning out to be.

The next morning I sat quietly while eating my breakfast, feeling tired after my restless night. Jean and I played hopscotch on the paved part of the farmyard. As I threw the flat stone along the ground, Jean asked me the dreaded question.

"Mary, why didn't your mum come?"

I thought for a brief moment then lied, "Er… she had to stay at home and help my dad."

I thought that sounded quite logical and I felt pleased with myself. Jean seemed satisfied with my reply and we continued our game. As the day progressed, I never asked about my mother and Aunt B never told me the real reason for Mum's absence. We had a very warm day and later there was a thunderstorm. Connie had hidden in the airing cupboard and just wouldn't come out. I liked the thunder and I peeped between the drawn curtains to watch God's patterns across the blackened sky. Aunt B said it sounded like the bombing in the war.

"Mary, why don't you do some drawing?"

I had forgotten about my new drawing book. I scrambled into the big chair and laid out my first page. I drew Aunt B as a stick person, which didn't seem to do her justice. I chewed on the end of my pencil in pensive thought. So, on the next page, I started to draw her as I really saw her: a smiling face, arms, body and legs with fullness and colour. Aunt B was impressed and I began to realise how much I enjoyed drawing after that day. To sit and sketch gave me enormous pleasure; I realise now, it was the best gift Dad could have ever given to me.

The next morning brought a fresh, sweet smell, after the previous day's downpour. As I ventured in the yard, I stared at the inviting dark puddles the rain had left behind. I was alone, except for one or two chickens pecking at my feet; all the children were at school. There was no wind and the pools were so still. I stared into one and saw a small, thin girl staring back at me. I threw a pebble and my reflection was gone. Slowly, I stepped along the edge of the pool, my arms outstretched as if balancing, treading fairy feet around it. Then, I slowly touched the centre of the puddle with my toe. I liked doing that. It was a magic pond and I would jump into the middle. I stepped away and, with all my might, I leapt into its centre, splashing water all around me. But the magic pond was becoming smaller and I was becoming wetter. My toes squelched inside my sand shoes, but I quite liked the feeling. I ran around and jumped into all the magic pools until they were all obliterated.

Aunt B came out, her basket resting on her hip; she was about to collect the eggs. I smiled up at her, but she wasn't amused. "Mary, you bad girl, you're wet through!"

"I've been jumping in the magic ponds, Auntie!"

"I'll give you magic, you naughty girl, ooh." She dragged me into the house, she was almost crying, she was so angry. Her eyes were big and menacing and I felt slightly afraid. She was about to slap me with the back of her hand, when I winced. She stopped herself, but she kept repeating how naughty I had been. I bit my lip with remorse and my wet feet were now beginning to feel rather cold. Aunt B let out a sigh of annoyance as she began to peel off my soggy clothes. I never said one word, as she quickly undressed me to my liberty bodice and my vest. That seemed to be the only dry part of my anatomy.

"Look at your dirty face," Aunt B snapped. She held out a hand mirror - my face was splattered with mud - then she pulled me towards the sink. "We have to save water, not waste it!" she shouted, as she sponged my grimy face. She wasn't gentle.

"No sweets for you this week. Don't you ever do that again, do you hear? Do you hear?"

"I… I'm really sorry," I mumbled.

"Well, I think you are now," she answered. She wrapped me in a large towel and spoke again as she pointed her finger at me, "Now don't move." Then she left me.

I sat there for what seemed an eternity while she went to collect the eggs. As I rubbed my tears away, I gazed at my muddied clothes on the wooden draining board; I had really made a mess and a lot of washing for Aunt B. I had never seen her angry like this before. I suppose it was thoughtless of me. I was only playing make believe, a silly game and the thought of no sweet ration….

When Auntie B came back, she dressed me in a tee-shirt and a pair of shorts. "They are a bit big, but they will have to do! You will wear these until your other clothes are washed." I felt humiliated in the large shorts. They hung below the level of my knees; that was punishment enough. I sat sheepishly in the corner of the room, not daring to move. Aunt B worked about quite noisily, glancing my way now and again. After a while, she tied an old apron around my waist and stood me on the milking stool by the sink. What punishment was this? Was she going to wash me again? She gave a deep sigh, "You can wash your own clothes."

I looked down into the large sink, it was bubbling with lather. I stared firstly at Aunt B and then at the dirty clothes. I didn't know where to start. Aunt B took my little blouse and dipped it in and out of the warm soap suds, brushing areas of the garment with a nail brush, on the draining board.

She nodded, "You do the same."

There seemed to be more soap on me than on my washing. The scrubbing seemed to take forever. Finally Aunt B rinsed all the suds away and showed me how to wring out the clothes. She wouldn't let me use the big mangle in the yard, saying that, 'I might trap my fingers'. Finally, we hung the washing on the line; this part I quite liked. Aunt B was sombre and I didn't give her cause for any more alarm. I was so quiet that she looked worried. She held out my drawing book. "Do you want to do some drawing Mary?"

"Yes, please," I answered with great politeness and, as I sat drawing the farm yard and the chickens, I felt a deep wave of repentance and stared up at Aunt B. "I'm really, really sorry, Auntie."

Aunt B put her head on one side and smiled. "Aye you're a rum lass! Never mind now, it's forgotten," and she quickly changed the subject.

"What are you drawing?" she smiled.

"The farm yard," I answered quickly, fumbling for a different colour.

"Well, don't forget the animals," she took a deep breath, "…and the puddles too." She laughed. The chuckle came from deep within her round frame. My heart lifted and a rush of tears filled my eyes. I quickly threw my arms around Auntie's waist and hugged her. Her hands rested on my shoulders. "I couldn't be vexed with you for long, some day you'll melt someone's heart with your winning ways, Mary and no mistake."

I didn't quite know what Auntie meant, but I did know that she felt as happy as I did at that very moment.

I suppose I was as mischievous as the next child, but I would never forget the magic pools.

I spent a lot of time alone, which led me to play make believe and my conversations with Betsy became a daily ritual. To her, I would spill my innermost thoughts, vowing a deepening hatred for my mother and an undying love for Aunt B. She was my best friend, but I never told her of my hatred for my mum.

Sunday was a cool, fresh morning. I went with Aunt B to church and we sang my favourite hymn, 'All creatures great and small'. I thought about all the wild flowers, the thrushes down the lane and all the farm animals. When we arrived back from church, I sat at the corner of the kitchen table and began to draw. My mouth watered as the aroma of roast beef danced in the warm steamy air. I decided to draw a picture of Connie. She seemed to be posing especially for me. Auntie liked my picture so much, that she pinned it up on the kitchen door, but she kept to her word; this was the one week I had no sweet ration, though she did give me some extra currants.

That day was the same as any other for the farmer and later that afternoon, Aunt B suggested that we go to the parlour to watch the cows being milked. I frowned. "They won't be milked today, Auntie, it is Sunday!"

A big grin came over her face and she laughed out loud, "Bless yer, love, they have to be milked every day, no matter what."

"But why, Auntie?"

"Well, because the cow produces milk every day and if the milk isn't taken away, the cows would be sore and poorly, so the farmer relieves them by taking away their milk regularly, twice a day - even Christmas day."

Some of the other children and I gathered around and watched. A few young men were sitting on milking stools, their heads pressed against the cows' flanks, some talking gently saying, 'Steady there girl, steady.'

Then that hollow sound came, as the first squirts of liquid hit the side of the galvanised buckets. Like magic, the milk frothed and bubbled, slowly easing the cows' discomfort. The cows were content and I could almost sing a tune to the alternate pinging against the metal and the young men whistling between their teeth, as they pulled on the greasy udders. I stood there enraptured. Jean and the others wanted to go, but I wanted to stay. Aunt B suggested that I could stay for a few more minutes and the other children ran away.

'How could the others be so bored?' I thought. As I watched, I was aware of one of the young men staring at me. I looked down at my toes, that feeling of shyness engulfing me.

"Hey!" shouted the young man. He had fair tousled hair, rosy cheeks and blue eyes. He sat back on his stool, resting.

"Haven't you seen a cow being milked a fore?"

My mouth was dry. "Err, no," I whispered.

"This is Violet. She's the best milker; gives us the most I reckon," and he patted her hard on her flank. Dust rose from her curly hide.

"Would you like a drink, of milk, I mean?" he laughed.

My eyes widened as I shouted, "Yes!" excitedly.

"Come closer then," he beckoned. I walked slowly towards him. When I was only a few feet away he shouted, "Here you are then!" He squeezed the udder hard and turned it in my direction. The hot white liquid showered my hair, seeping into my eyes and I threw up my hands in horror, screaming. The young man laughed aloud, as I turned on my heels and ran. He hadn't hurt me, I was just humiliated.

Aunt B was sat darning some socks. "Good girl, you didn't stay too long." But she frowned when she saw me. I had tide marks on my face from my tears and the front of my dress was wet and sticky. "Oh, have you been in puddles again?" she moaned.

"Aunt B, he sprayed the milk at me," I cried.

She smiled. "Oh that will be Tom, up to his old tricks again. He's a bit cheeky, but it's only his fun."

"I hate him," I shouted indignantly through my tears. Aunt B stroked my dishevelled, damp hair.

"Never mind, pet, but you don't really hate him. It's very bad to say you hate someone, you must never say that. He did something naughty, but you must never hate him for that. Hate is a bad word, it's very final. You maybe don't like him at this moment because you are cross, but you don't hate him."

I suppose Aunt B was right, she was always right. After I had washed and dressed, Aunt B gave me a glass of milk and I calmed down. Apart from my milky initiation, I enjoyed being at the milk parlour.

As I lay in bed that evening I talked to Betsy once more. "I watched the cows being milked today, Betsy. One cow was called Violet. I wonder how Tom knew her. They all look the same to me!"

I thought of what Aunt B had said and I felt very guilty. The many times I had said how I had hated my mother; I was beginning to think that I was wrong. I put my palms together and said a little prayer, "Please God, I'm sorry if I hated my mum, but I don't like her very much, but please look after my mam and dad and let me see them soon," I paused and screwed up my nose, "and can I have some new crayons?"

Chapter 4
'Brandy'

The next day, a man called to see Aunt B. They sat in the kitchen, talking. He wasn't a farm labourer; he wore a smart suit and his facial expressions were like that of Aunt B. I think he might have been her brother. With him was this large Labrador dog. His name was 'Brandy'. He was very friendly and he ignored Connie, who instinctively hunched her back and hissed in a most intolerant manner.

After that day, Brandy stayed at the farm and we immediately became great friends. When I asked Auntie about him, she said she was looking after the dog while the man visited a friend, who had been hurt in the war. I reflected for a brief moment; at times I completely forgot about the war. I was so happy there and only a few miles away from the air raids, which were a common occurrence.

It was great fun to have Brandy. Aunt B would let me take him for long walks. We ran together in the fields and chased cabbage whites and red admiral butterflies as they hovered above our heads. The summer school holidays began and that meant that I could spend more time with my new friend, Jean. She taught me how to play lots of games, especially with a tennis ball. Games like 'Queeny' and 'Donkey', but 'Double Ball' was the most demanding and it was my favourite. Although I was only five, I seemed to take to it like a circus juggler. Sometimes we would play 'Hop Scotch' or 'Jacks', the latter being a game of sleight-of-hand. We skipped often, even though I couldn't seem to co-ordinate my feet with the rope, but every day, Jean and I would end up in the barn playing 'Cat's Cradle' with our grubby string. Brandy loved the other children and would follow us everywhere.

One day, the boys tied a rope to his collar and stood astride him, pretending he was a horse, then, suddenly, Jean came up with an idea. "Brandy could give us a ride," she shouted gleefully. The boys huddled together, whispering, then they all stared towards me.

Raymond, the biggest of the boys, looked up. "Hey, Mary, how would you like a ride?" and without waiting for my reply, he dashed into the barn and produced a rickety looking box with small pram wheels protruding from each corner. Quickly, he tied the rope from Brandy to the front of the box. He then turned in my direction. "Come on, you can be first 'cause you're the smallest." Everyone stared my way.

"No! I don't want to," I scoffed.

"Of course you do, it'll be fun," Raymond persisted.

"No!" I shouted defiantly. The others started to jeer and taunt. "She's a baby, a baby!"

That made me angry; no one was going to call me a baby, so I scrambled into the box quickly. I stared at the old rope and tried to grab the sides of the wood and I swallowed hard.

"Hold on!" shouted Raymond, holding his hand high.

During all this banter, Brandy stood quietly watching, his tongue lolling from his mouth, his ears twitching. With all his might, Raymond threw a small stick. "Fetch it, Brandy, fetch it!" And everyone cheered.

No sooner had he uttered the words, Brandy set off at a gallop. My makeshift carriage wrenched forward and I toppled head-first like a ball out of a cannon. The upturned box was dragged along the ground as I toppled, slowly coming to a stop, hitting the edge of a sharp stone along the path.

The pain didn't start at first. There was a lot of screaming and Jean was kneeling beside me. There seemed to be a red haze around me. Jean's face appeared very close to mine; she looked concerned.

"You'll be all right, I'll fetch Auntie Betty."

My head felt quite numb, but suddenly, a searing, sharp pain stung my knee and brought me to my senses. With my sore hands, I clasped at my leg and I saw blood oozing from a gash across my knee cap. Raymond was wide-eyed.

"Is it broken?" he whispered.

"Ow... Ow, I don't know!" I cried and I cried. Everyone stood around me, staring in stunned silence. The only sound I could hear was Brandy panting. Raymond's eyes grew bigger as he stared at my crumpled skin.

"Gosh, yer bleeding," he mumbled.

I could hear Aunt B's voice: "Move out of the way," she yelled at the others, rushing towards me, staring. "Oh, Mary, what have you done? Dear, dear," she sighed. She held her warm hands and cupped them around my face.

"They made me ride, Auntie," I sobbed.

"Never mind about that, where does it hurt, love?"

"My knee, my knee!" I cried and Auntie B quickly took off her apron and turned it wrong side up. She folded it into a make-shift bandage and gently wrapped it round my leg, then she gently lifted me up and took me indoors.

First, she bathed my grazed forehead and hands. "Now, let's have a look at this knee," she whispered. The blood had seeped through all the layers of apron and Aunt B looked quite anxious.

"Umm, we'll have to take you to the hospital, pet, it's a deep cut, it may need stitches."

In fact, Aunt B knew that it needed stitches, but she didn't want to frighten me. Jean was watching from the doorway.

"Shall I find Tom?" she shouted.

Aunt B looked up. "Yes, love, tell him to bring the truck." Tom came within seconds.

"Tom, would you take us to hospital, Mary's hurt her leg?"

"Do I really have to go, Auntie?" I begged.

"Yes, pet, they will make it better."

"What will they do?" I asked, feeling afraid.

"They will bandage it up," she replied. I thought that Aunt B could have done that.

As Tom carried me towards the hospital doors, I could smell carbolic and I felt a bit sick.

"Have yer been in hospital afore?" Tom smiled.

"No," I whispered, feeling scared.

"Don't be frightened, Mary, the nurses are all very kind and when yer knee's better, yer can come to the barn and see Violet again. I promise I won't squirt milk at yer," he laughed.

We went into a cubical and Tom sat me on a white covered bed. Aunt B sat beside me and held my hand whispering, "It will soon be better, love."

I would have been extremely rich if I had had a penny for every tear I had shed that day. I had six stitches and there were horrible injections, the first one to numb the area, then the second - that was the worst, it was in my bottom! 'Tetanus', Aunt B called it.

As Tom drove me back to the farm, Aunt B held me close in her arms and said that I could sleep in her room that night. The next day, I felt very sore and stiff. I hardly dared to put my weight on my bad leg. Aunt B let me sit on the easy chair by the Aga cooker and she propped my leg on a cushion, on the milking stool. I began to feel quite important. When all the boys came to visit me, I proudly showed them my bandaged knee and, of course, I told them of my whole six stitches.

Like any child, I enjoyed being the centre of attention. Each day my leg improved and an ugly scab formed on my forehead. It itched so much that I wanted to pick it, but Auntie stopped me and said that was a sign that it was getting better. Auntie let me stay with her for quite a few days and I was able to do lots of drawings for her to put up on the kitchen walls. I especially enjoyed creating a picture for the doctor's surgery. I limped around the house and my leg became stronger, but Aunt B held my hand as I ventured through the yard.

It was Tuesday morning and I was just tucking into my second slice of toast. Aunt B smiled. "Mary, you are having your stitches out today, dear," then she continued to drink her tea.

My face dropped in shock and I felt scared. I frowned, "Why do they take stitches out when they have been put in?"

Aunt B sniffed and looked upwards for inspiration. "Well, pet, the stitches are put in to mend your cut; your skin then heals by itself. That's why they are taken out, because they are not needed anymore. They are a little like tacking stitches."

I rubbed my chin. "Oh," I said thoughtfully, "but it might bleed again, Auntie."

She laughed. "No, love, your skin has now fused together and is getting better. It may be a little sore when they take the stitches out, but that won't last for long."

One thing about Auntie B, she was always honest with me. Tom gave us a lift into the village and we went to the local surgery. As I sat in the waiting room, the loud tick of the clock on the wall beckoned. I sighed and tried to be brave. Highly polished chairs circled an oval coffee table, strewn with 'Woman's Weeklies', 'Titbits', and 'Dandy' and 'Beano' comics. I fumbled through a comic, but Dan Dare's antics didn't seem funny at all. I kept looking towards the bell on the wall, waiting for its inevitable piercing ring and thinking of my great entrance to the spotless, disinfected room. Finally, the door opened and a young girl with short-cropped, wavy hair smiled at me.

"Miss Thompson, Mary, you can come in now, dear."

I gulped as Aunt B led me through the frosted glass doorway. The room was rather cluttered -not what I had imagined. There were lots of pictures on the walls of men on horseback and groups of Indians. Sat in front of me was a bald-headed man, distinctly red-faced. He had a small moustache, pale blue eyes and deep lines on his forehead. He looked very old. His white shirt sleeves were rolled up to his elbows and his grey waistcoat sported a fob chain across his chest. He didn't wear a white coat at all.

"Hello, Mary, isn't it?" he said in a gentle voice. I nodded shyly, Aunt B handed him a note from the hospital and, after propping a pair of rimless spectacles on the end of his nose, he proceeded to read it. I was so quiet; I could almost hear my own heartbeat. Aunt B nodded to me and smiled as if giving me courage.

"Mm," the doctor sighed. "Right, my dear, can you sit up here?" he asked, patting the long black Rexine sofa. I watched him as he slowly unravelled the wide bandage; towards the last few inches, I could feel it sticking to my skin. He must have felt my anguish; he turned and looked at me with a deep, meaningful smile. "This may sting a little. Are you a brave girl, Mary?"

I almost replied, 'Of course', but I was more cautious. "I … I don't know," I whispered.

As he talked, he gently prised the gauze from my scabbed wound. It hurt, but I gripped my hands together, showing white knuckles. I was quite shocked at the large scar before me. The doctor frowned and looked at me.

"How did you do this?"

"I was having a ride in a box," I answered quickly. The doctor frowned even more.

Aunt B continued to explain, "You know how children are, Doctor. They had a home-made go-cart and Mary fell out of it."

The doctor grinned, shaking his head. "I'm going to take the stitches out now, Mary."

Suddenly, I found some nerve. "Will it hurt?" I asked earnestly. The doctor looked at my leg, then he lifted his glasses and pulled them down to the bridge of his nose. He stared deep into my eyes and shook his head.

"Do you ever play 'Cat's Cradle', Mary?"

My eyes widened even more. "Why yes all the time, with my friend Jean." How did he know, I wondered?

He smiled. "Well, if I gave you a long piece of string to hold and you gripped it tightly in your fingers and I pulled that string away from you, your fingers would hurt, wouldn't they?"

"Yes," I frowned.

"But," he continued, "if you loosened your grasp and I pulled it from you, it wouldn't hurt at all, would it?"

Confused, I whispered, "No."

"So, if you try to relax, it won't hurt." He smiled again as he pushed his glasses back in place, then he pulled the first thin thread of catgut. I looked away and tried to relax.

"Your Auntie told me that you like to draw, Mary."

"Oh, yes, I draw the farm and all the animals."

"Will you draw a picture for me and I'll put it in my surgery?"

"Yes," I said, proudly. The doctor beamed.

"That's it! All out! You were a brave girl, Mary."

I realised that all the while he was conversing with me, he was beavering away, taking out the stitches. I smiled with relief and felt a little pleased with myself. The doctor continued to bandage the area.

"Keep it clean, Mary and in a day or two, you will be as right as rain; though I wouldn't ride any go-carts if I were you," he laughed. He was a wise and gentle man and I never forgot about the 'Cat's Cradle'. Aunt B gave me a hug as we turned to go. The doctor leaned over his desk.

"Just a minute." He opened a small drawer and took out a small brown paper bag, which he held out to me. "Here, have a jelly baby for being a good girl."

"Gosh, my favourite," I gasped.

In the days that followed, I hobbled about and my knee became stronger. I was helping Aunt B hang out the washing when she told me, so calmly. The shock was so great that I stared into space, a dripping towel in my shaking hands. Aunt B repeated herself.

"Mary! Did you hear what I said? Hey! Anybody there?" She was squatting down beside me in the grass.

"Mary, yer mum is coming to see you, aren't you pleased? You see, pet, I sent your mum a letter. Had to tell her about your accident and I received a reply this morning. She's coming in the next day or two."

The pain I felt was worse than my fall. A feeling of hate, guilt, and frustration ate at my stomach. My senses seemed to reel. I thought about my mother; I didn't know her anymore. She was a stranger.

"She won't come, I know she won't," I shouted, angrily. I stood on the spot, thumped my sides with my fists and screamed and screamed hysterically until I felt a resounding slap on the side of my face. I stopped suddenly and caught my breath. Aunt B had never smacked me before. She bit her bottom lip as I fell into her arms, sobbing. She stroked my hair until my shaking body became calm.

"Come along, pet, let's hang out the washing."

Chapter 5
'Mam!'

That night, I sat in the barn with Jean. She showed me her cigarette card collection and she taught me how to flick the cards along the ground. The pictures were of all different film stars.

I decided to write and ask my dad to save all the cards from his cigarette packets. Then we played 'Cat's Cradle' once more. I didn't tell Jean about my mother coming in case she didn't turn up. That night proved a restless one for me, I felt so confused. I really did want to see my mother, but I had no idea what I was going to say to her. The next morning, Tom came to the kitchen; he smiled.

"Hello, Mary, now that you're feeling better, I thought that you would like to come to the milking tonight, at around five o clock."

"Yes, please," I beamed.

So, as I helped Aunt B that day, I was counting the hours and minutes to five o'clock. Later, Auntie let me walk to the milk parlour on my own. I stood silently and listened to the tuneful turbulence of the milk filling the bright zinc buckets.

As Tom looked up, I pointed to the cow nearest to me and asked him, "Is this Violet?"

"Yes," he replied, "would you like to milk her?"

I nodded excitedly. Cautiously, I stepped towards Tom and the cow. Tom laughed.

"Don't worry." He gestured for me to squat on the small stool. Violet quivered, turned and mooed at me. She looked so huge and I felt so vulnerable. Tom squatted down behind me, putting both his arms around my body. He pressed the palms of my hands against the cow's udders. They felt funny, like soft warm balloons.

He motioned to me. "Now squeeze, like this." We pulled gently in one long movement. Then Tom stepped back. "Now you do it."

I tried, but not much milk came at first, but after a few attempts, the pail began to fill. Violet turned her head and eyed me once more and she mooed again.

"She must know it's not you, Tom," I whispered.

"I reckon she knows everything we say, Mary, shall I carry on now?"

I willingly forfeited my spot on the stool. Apart from my hands feeling very greasy, I was afraid that Violet might kick me, as she seemed to be becoming a little restless. Now I could tell everyone that I had milked a cow and I was only five!

As Jean and I sat in the barn that night, Jean was excited.

"Can I see yer knee again?" she whispered quickly. I pulled up the hem of my dress and she took a long look.

"Golly, will that scar be there forever?"

"Yes," I answered proudly, not realising that this night would be our last time together and 'Cat's Cradle' would be nought but a fond memory.

I felt more relaxed that evening and sleep soon came. Aunt B decided to wash my hair the following morning. I didn't like the ritual of the shampooing. At least Aunt B used a proper shampoo named 'Amaimi'. My mum used ordinary carbolic soap, which took ages to rinse off; but no matter how it was done, I never liked rinsing my hair, it always stung my eyes for ages. Aunt B told me I must look after my hair, or I would get nits. Nits were tiny eggs which lived on the strands of one's hair, so I was told. They turned into little creatures no bigger than a pin head. The nits passed from one strand of hair to another. I think that is why Aunt B always put my hair into a plait or tied it in a ribbon, so I wouldn't have an itchy head.

It was to be two more days before my mother came. I first caught sight of her beyond a field, a small trim figure, growing larger, coming closer. I stood, transfixed, as I watched her walking down the lane towards the farm. I could hear her light step on the gravel as it crunched under her feet, her patent leather court shoes so unsuitable for the terrain. A pillbox hat perched above her dark curls, her round face pale under her rouge-tinted cheeks. Her trim figure flattered a blue serge suit. She also wore a blouse with fly-away collar lolling over the wide lapels, a white shoulder bag swinging with her gait. I couldn't explain my feelings at that moment. Why should I feel so apprehensive and afraid? She was my mother and she loved me. The next few hours were to be the worst of my life.

I ran behind the barn door and tried to gather my thoughts. I didn't run to her; I wanted to, but my body wouldn't. Mum hadn't seen me, so I sat, hiding, in the corner of the barn. They were the longest minutes I had ever known. There was this smell of Ashes of Roses as she passed by the barn door. My mind was devoid of excitement and I felt tears well up inside me as I craved love and tenderness from a mum who, in my eyes, didn't seem to care. I lifted up my string and patterned the criss-cross of the 'Cat's Cradle' between my hot sticky fingers, pretending I didn't know of Mum's existence. After a few moments, Aunt B appeared in the doorway.

"Mary! Mary!" she shouted.

"Yes, Auntie." My voice was shaky. I stood up and looked into the light of the doorway. Aunt B's arms were outstretched, beckoning to me.

"Come along, your mum is here."

I walked towards her slowly, dreading this moment. She smiled, held my hand and led me towards the house. My mother sat beside the kitchen table, her gold compact wedged in her left palm, her right hand dabbing her nose with a powder puff. She quickly clasped the compact shut.

"Hello, love." She was smiling.

I wanted to run to her, but my feet wouldn't move. My mouth was dry and I groped for words, but could only manage a weak smile. She came towards me.

"It hasn't been long, but I do think you've grown, Mary." Her perfume wafted deep into my nostrils, I felt her netted gloved hands firmly on my shoulders. She stared wildly into my eyes.

"Have you lost your voice, then?"

"I thought you wouldn't come, Mam."

"Oh, as cheeky as ever, but let's have a look at your leg, is it better?" At this remark I proudly looked down at my scarred knee and Mum looked too.

"My God!" she exclaimed, somewhat shocked, "whatever were you doing?"

At this point Aunt B butted in. "She was riding in a go-cart, Mrs Thompson and she fell out."

At this remark my mum swung round and turned on Aunt B. "So it's your fault. You're not capable of looking after children. It's disgraceful, we're not staying here another minute, Mary we're going home."

"But, Mam!" I shouted in astonishment.

Aunt B tried to calm her. "You've come a long way; I'll make us a cup of tea."

Mum's voice was high pitched, "I don't want your tea. Mary, get your things, we're going back to Hull."

I couldn't believe what I was hearing. I pulled away from Mum and clung tightly to Aunt B's skirt.

"No, I don't want to," I cried and Aunt B stroked my hair as I sobbed uncontrollably. She looked very serious.

"All the children in my care are well looked after. You can't do this! Mary is happy here! She had an accident; these things happen. Mary has settled down here and made friends, she loves the farm."

My mother butted in, clearly in a rage. I remember seeing her like this when she once had a row with my dad. She took no notice of Aunt B's words and pulled on my arm.

"Where are the rest of your clothes? I want your gas mask and your case now. NOW!" Her voice was now a terrible screech. I looked up at Aunt B and I felt that I could never leave her. My mother was clearly out of her mind; maybe war did that to people. I jumped as my mother defiantly pounded the kitchen table with her fist.

"Mary, we're going now!" Her voice rasped in my ears as I saw her glazed hysterical expression. I looked from one to the other.

"Please, Auntie, I want to stay here."

Aunt B crouched down and looked onto my eyes.

"If your mum wants to take you, love, you'll have to go. I don't want you to go, but I can't stop your mum from taking you back home." Aunt B's face was flushed and unhappy, "I'll get your things together," and she fled from the room, close to tears. My mother sank back into the chair gritting her teeth.

"It's for the best, Mary," she added.

"I hate you, I hate you, I'm not leaving Aunt B!" I screamed through my tears.

I ran quickly past my mother and through the kitchen door. I ran and ran, not knowing where I was going and then I became out of breath. I found myself in a field and I fell to my knees in the long grass.

How I wished at that moment that I could have turned into a bird and flown away, high over the hills and my mother would have gone back home. I would have flown back and perched on Aunt B's window-sill, then I would have turned into myself again. I felt so wretched and unhappy.

It was quiet here as I sat among the daisies and the buttercups and I remembered the afternoon that my mum didn't come; it was only to be a reprieve. A child has only basic perceptions, but if I had to leave Aunt B, I wanted to die.

When I finally came to my senses, I felt rather cold. I must have been asleep. It was quite dark and there was this ringing sound in my head. I shivered as I realised how alone I was. The grass felt damp with dew and crickets buzzed along the stalks. I had no idea where I was, but I knew that I wanted to go back to Aunt B; I then remembered my mother would be there. I couldn't see the daisies and buttercups anymore and, as I walked, I fumbled in the darkness. I was feeling dejected, cold and a little afraid. It would have been so nice to have been tucked up in my bed, hugging Betsy. I kept rubbing my fist across my eyes, as the tears kept forming in my distress. My body quivered and, as darkness enveloped me, I started to talk.

"Mum will never find me in the dark." I was consoled with that thought, but I grimaced as I realised my futile predicament. I felt so cold. There seemed to be a black fog in front of my eyes. Suddenly, I saw a light ahead, it seemed to move and then was swallowed up in the deep blackness.

"I must be near to a road," I cried. I had no money, not even a coat, I had run away in such haste. Yet, I had shown my feelings to be strong and aggressive. I shuddered and gave a long broken sigh. Deep down inside I knew it was all so useless. There was this light again and this time, I heard voices, men's voices.

"Mary! Mary!" The lights I had seen were torches. I could see this shadow walking towards me; it was Tom. My crying ceased, I felt so happy to hear a familiar voice, I couldn't stop shaking.

"Tom," I croaked and many sounds echoed through the air, the wind and the crickets resounded in my head, everything was so loud. The soft wet grass touched my face as I collapsed in sheer exhaustion.

When I opened my eyes, everybody's face looked hazy, like when the sun is shining so brightly that outlines cannot be seen. I saw Mum's face first; she didn't speak, she just stared into my eyes. Then I saw Aunt B, she was smiling. I think she had been crying, her eyes looked red.

"Pet, you're alright now." She held out a beaker of warm milk. Mum fussed above my head, poking and patting the propped-up pillows.

"Why did you run away, you silly girl?" Mum's face was serious. I didn't answer, but I smiled as I picked up Betsy and held her close. My mum was about to scold me again, but Aunt B shushed her and they quietly left the room. The milk tasted magic and briefly, I smiled at Betsy. Then I remembered I would have to go home and I whimpered a doleful sigh, feeling so sad.

"Oh, Betsy, I'm sleeping here for the last time," and I sobbed into my pillow. I gripped my hands into a fist and began to pray.

"Dear God, I'm too tired to say much, but I ask one thing of you. Please look after Aunt B when I go away. I will always love her," and I quietly sobbed myself to sleep. This was a time of great sadness for me, but the trauma of this episode in my life made me grow from a weak, puny child, to a tenacious one. I had to accept the way my life had to be. The war took away a child's idyllic thoughts and optimism. I was resilient and no matter what, I would survive.

After the following morning, I was never to see Aunt B again. To me, she would always be the kindest, most loving person I had ever met. Some of her kindness seemed to rub off on Mum, for her attitude towards me became gentler, less impatient. On that final morning, breakfast was a very subdued affair. My small case and gas mask stood beside the kitchen door and the atmosphere was tinged with unhappiness. My mother sipped her tea in orderly fashion and I toyed with my spoon in my porridge and craned my head to see if I could see Connie on the window sill. There was so much I would miss. As I walked towards the lane, gas mask box hung around my chest and holding my attaché case, Aunt B pressed a small paper carrier into my hands; her eyes were misty and my body shook once more with sobs.

"These are your drawings and crayons and some of your favourite scones in there too." I gripped her warm thighs.

"Aunt B," I cried. I couldn't say the word, 'goodbye'. "I'll love you forever."

Aunt B gave a broken sigh, "Oh, pet, do take care and keep up your drawing, Mary." Her voice sounded strained. Mum waited silently; she knew that I needed some moments of solace. I needed to reflect on the farm, Connie, Brandy, Tom, my new friend Jean and all the others.

"I'll come back one day," I whispered through my tears. Aunt B was holding my hands in hers, they were hot and sweaty, like the first day when she lifted me up off the station platform. Then she loosened her grip and Mum pulled me away from her. Our arms were outstretched as we left one another's side. My sobs were stifling me, as Mum fussed and tried to dab away my tears. I could feel her hand in mine as she pulled me towards the lane. My head was turned in Aunt B's direction until she became smaller and I saw her mouth the word, 'Goodbye'.

The moment I had been dreading was now here and it hurt so much.

Soon the figure of Aunt B, Tom, Jean, the farm, everything, my whole world, were fading away. I turned around and took a deep breath, trying to dispel my feeling of sickness as I hobbled along in helpless fashion. Soon we neared the bus stop and, after a long few minutes, Mum spoke.

"Here I'll tek that," and she reached for my paper carrier.

"No," I shouted in deep despair, "it's mine." I hugged the carrier close to my body, as if I were hugging Betsy. "Aunt B gave it to me."

The carrier could have been made of gold, so precious were its contents. Mum shrugged her shoulders and instead, she lifted the small suitcase from my hands, then we walked on quietly. We stood at the end of the crossroads and awaited our bus.

There was no one else around, but the cows were grazing nearby and larks feathered the air, high above our heads. It was a beautiful day, the sun shone and a faint breeze whistled through the hawthorn hedgerows. All this life about me and I felt numb, deprived of all feeling. I just stared through smarting eyes as the space around me was bereft.

Mum was grumbling about the bus being late, her voice carried in the wind. When the bus did arrive, my body jumped. I had to will myself to climb onto the running board.

Mum smiled. "Come along, Mary, you can sit by the window if you like."

So I did as I was told. My head was bowed and I stared at the dusty bus floor, counting the discarded bus tickets. The journey was short and soon we arrived at the railway station. I read out the name, 'Selby'. We walked into an echoing waiting room; it was all treacle brown paint and bright brass door knobs. We sat on a long bench and waited. I didn't speak, but I heard Mum give a doleful sigh.

"Well, I didn't know you would be coming home with me; your dad will be surprised."

I looked up into her wild eyes; I stared hard for a long time and I felt that I hated and despised her for being my mother. She cleared her throat and looked away, feeling uncomfortable; she had never seen me like this before. We both sat with our thoughts, in silence, the only sound to be heard was the guard, his footsteps tapping in the distance. The atmosphere was heavy with a barrier of unhappiness. My mum tried to make conversation.

"Do you still have your little felt doll, Mary?"

I just answered politely, "Yes," as I gently lifted the string handles of my carrier and peeped at the little doll, dressed all in pink. I folded my arms across my knees and held the carrier tightly, almost crushing its contents. My head bowed. I caught sight of Mum's legs; her once shiny black patent leather shoes were now dusty, scuffed and dull. She sat cross-legged, one foot on the paved floor, the other leg slightly swinging. Her bare skin was quite pink with the fiery blood pumping through her veins. A tuft of white lace peeped from under her pleated skirt and creases ran along the seams to her thin waist, which was hugged by a wide black wasp belt. A white chiffon blouse delicately caressed her small breasts and the large collar sported a lace trim. Her short box jacket covered small shoulders and the stiffened collar at her neck hid her dark curls. Her features were set, frowning, with black eyebrow pencil, too heavy, above her eye lids. She had tiny green eyes, their dark pupils almost like pin heads, which made them look almost like those of a rabid animal.

Her lids kept closing, as if she needed sleep. Her skin was pale and her mouth thin, tight, shut, waiting .Then I stared at the long hat pin as it pushed its way through the blue felt of her pillbox hat. She had a delicate beauty when she wasn't angry. A faint hissing could be heard and Mum and I walked onto the platform. It was hard to differentiate my feelings from the last time I had been here, when I was desolate and unhappy. Once again, I felt almost the same, only now, in only three months, I had aged much more than my five years. A few people hastily stepped along the platform and pulled themselves into the coaches.

"Hurry, Mary, we don't want him to go without us, do we?" Mum muttered. I wished he would.

We had a coach to ourselves. I was able to look out of either side of the carriage and within only two minutes we were moving along, the train chauffeuring, gathering speed. I sat quietly, my precious carrier balanced carefully on my knees. Mum fidgeted in her white sling bag and pulled out a tube of Rowntree's Fruit Gums; she offered them to me. I took a dark-red gum and sucked hard as the countryside breezed past. I thought that we had travelled hundreds of miles, but it was only about forty.

The hour on that train seemed an eternity. Neither of us had spoken and, as Mum kept looking towards me smiling, I began to mellow. I was thinking so much of Aunt B and all she had said to me, 'You must never hate; hate is a bad word'. The train seemed to whisper the words to me, "You must never hate, you must never hate, you must never hate."

How could I hate my mother? After all, she was only doing what she thought was best for me. We pulled into Paragon Station on a late July afternoon, it was 1940.

Chapter 6
'Dismay and Happiness'

Mum struggled with the large leather strap on the carriage door, let down the window and waited for the train to stop. She climbed down and helped me onto the platform. We walked along in the bustle of passengers towards the ticket barrier. I felt that the farm was a million miles away.

"Your tickets, please?" the guard was repeating in a firm, jolly voice.

The air was heavy with the smell of cinders and smoke and steam belched through our bodies as we filed past the huge green engine. Soldiers, workmen and turbaned women all thronged the platform: a crawling mass of humanity going about their business, their din echoing under the high glass canopy of the station roof.

After handing over our tickets, we walked briskly outside into the air. This wasn't country air; smoke seemed to hover around and there was a smell of charcoal. The pavements were wet, but not with rain, it was water from fire hydrants, which the firemen had used to dowse fire-bombs at various buildings. Many shops had broken windows. Burst water mains bubbled through cracked pavements and coloured ribbons were strewn across half-damaged buildings to keep the public at bay.

It seemed like an assault course as we walked towards the bus terminal in Jameson Street, where we waited in yet another queue. I stared upward; the bright blue sky had gone, and dull smoky clouds lathered the skies, as a watery sun clambered for space. There must have been a raid last night. I watched in silence as everyone seemed to accept everything around them; it was probably a normal day.

Along came our number 62 trolley bus, with the words, 'Newland Avenue' printed under the number at the front of the bus, just above the driver's window. The driver quickly negotiated the stop and switched off the power. These buses were powered by electricity and an overhead cable hovered in the space above them.

We finally boarded the bus, while the driver and the conductor took a last drag on their cigarettes as they watched our weary bodies and soon we were on our way. The bus was rather full, so I stood along the running board. I was swaying with the motion of the trolley, its power humming louder and louder, gathering speed, only to slow down again at every stop. Then the 'ping-ping' of the bell motioned the driver onward. We were squeezed closely together and I could smell body odour. As I stared at people's faces and beyond the grubby, fingered glass, there was this greyness, this faded memory of my way home: Spring Bank, Princes Avenue, then on to Newland Avenue. Mum pressed the bell as Goddard Avenue came into view.

We stepped off the bus and walked quickly down our avenue. Our terrace was named 'Alandale' and our house was the only one around that had been converted from gas to electricity, though gas points still adorned the walls. Mum didn't bother to produce her key, she pushed her palm through the letter box and pulled out a long string, on which hung the spare. The door stuck as she pushed her toe against the wooden panelling.

The passage was dark and uninviting and my first recollection of home was the smell of candle grease, 'Oxidol' and 'Brilliantine'. The front room housed a brown hide suite and a maple piano, with candlesticks protruding from the front panel. A vase of plastic roses sat on a plant stand in the large bay window. The floor was covered in mottled, brown-patterned linoleum and a tan, half-moon rug edged the dark wooden fireplace. The fireplace was majestic and tall, with alcoves at either side; a large oval mirror peered down from its centre. This room was hardly ever used. Mum called it our parlour, or the best room for visitors.

The next room was the living room; here we spent most of our time. It was also the warmest room. A drab coconut mat stretched out across its floor. Standing upon it was a square table, with three dining chairs tucked under its barley sugar legs. There was a wooden-armed fireside chair and a fat, shiny sideboard, on top of which laid an embroidered cover, an ashtray, a red glass fruit bowl and two picture frames of family members: grandmas and granddads. At the end of the sideboard, our rented 'Rediffusion' wireless stood. The black 'Yorkist' fireplace gleamed with Mum's generous black lead and the shafts of wood and old newspapers were tucked tidily in place, ready to be lit with the strike of a match. A grey fireguard stood like a sentry around the magnificent, strong iron grate and oven door and you could almost see your reflection in the deep red-tiled hearth.

There was a small step into the kitchen, though Mum always called it the scullery. In the corner, by the door, was a large, square, brown porcelain sink, around which Mum had hung a red check gingham curtain on a wire and one dull brass tap leaned out of the wall, dripping annoyance at our intrusion.

Along the wall to the right, stood a bath with a large brick copper inset into the corner. On the top of the bath, there was a hinged pine lid. Sometimes, I would lift up the lid just a touch and find a giant spider, spread-eagled inside the dusty bath bottom. I took a deep breath: the smell of home.

I could smell Dad; his overcoat was hung on the door. I caressed it and longed to see him again. Mum switched on the wireless; she then put the kettle on the stove. She was quiet and I was too and, to the soft drone of the Palm Court Orchestra, I started to look in my old toy box. I felt a feverish excitement within me as I thought of all the toys I hadn't seen for so long. While Mum set the table for tea, I sat on my little chair near to the gas cupboard and sorted through my toy box, feeling like I was seeing my toys for the first time.

"It's beans on toast for tea! Is that okay, Mary?" Mum asked from the kitchen.

And, as I replied, "Yes", I was beginning to feel quite hungry. And only this morning I had lost the will to do anything, let alone eat!

"Where's Dad, Mam?" I whispered. Her voice was muffled, as the kettle whistled.

"He's at work, but he will be home soon."

As I ate my toast, I wondered what I would have been eating had I been at Aunt B's; probably hot sweet scones and homemade jam. Suddenly, I heard the click of the back door and Dad was in the room. He stared across the table in great surprise.

"Mary, are you alright?" He hadn't even greeted Mum, he was so shocked.

Mum answered quickly, "She's fine, Jack. I decided to bring her back home."

"Dad!" I shouted, almost dragging the table cloth with me, "Dad!"

I ran to him and pulled on his neck. Dad laughed.

"Ouch, you'll choke me."

He scooped me up in his strong arms. I could smell the leaded paint from his overalls. I felt the 'Brilliantine' on his hair and the stubble on his chin.

"Oh, Dad," I sighed.

"My little bird," he cried and we held each other close in a frenzied cuddle and the foul stench of his overalls was like the smell of roses at that moment. There was a magic when I was with him. I could talk with him, he was patient and he always listened, he was so different from my mother. He was blessed with patience. He stepped back and held both his hands on my shoulders. "Let's look at you; I think you've grown, Mary, you're taller; but didn't you like the farm?"

Mum dropped Dad's knife and fork down hard on the table, as she almost screamed to butt-in.

"Err, I wanted her home with me." I looked into her face: she was flustered, agitated.

"Look at my knee, Dad!" I shouted, as I balanced on one leg, holding onto the back of the chair.

Then, to my surprise, Mum shouted even louder. "That's nothing! It's better now isn't it?" Mum's face was very red as she inhaled deeply. I frowned and I realised Mum wasn't going to tell him the real reason I was back home. It certainly wasn't for nothing; it was all because of my mum's fit of temper.

"Aunt B was ever so nice, Dad. She told me all about the farm and baked cakes and things and there was this big cat, and I milked a cow and…"

"Tell your father after tea, Mary," Mum butted in.

I sighed, sat back at the table and finished my cold beans. I watched as Dad took off his white overalls and hung them on the back of the kitchen door. He smiled at me through tired eyes.

"It was windy on that chair today, Eth," he muttered to my mother.

I looked puzzled. "Have you been sitting on a chair all day, Dad?"

Dad smiled, amused by my lack of understanding. "Well Mary, it's called a 'Bosun's chair'. I'm painting the side of a big ship and I'm sat on this contraption and it looks like a chair cum platform. It's hung over the side of the hull of the ship and that's how I am able to reach the area to paint."

"Is it high up, Dad?" I asked wide- eyed.

"Yes, but I'm strapped in, so I'm quite safe."

"Gosh," I whispered.

"There's a bit of bacon with your beans, Jack," Mum gestured, as she dished out Dad's food on his plate, "Your dad's painting one of His Majesty's ships for the war." I detected a note of pride in her voice. Dad nodded wearily and pecked Mum's cheek, but she edged away. I frowned.

"But it was warm today, Dad."

"I know, love," he grinned, as he sipped his tea, "but you get that cold wind from the River Humber."

I thought my dad was quite handsome. He had a sallow complexion and big brown eyes, a straight sculpted nose and thin lips. His hair was jet black and very shiny. He would brush his hair with two brushes, then make a side-parting and press his fingers along his head to make a wave. He was thin, but he was strong, kind and gentle. As Dad tucked into his tea, Mum stared at me. I could almost feel her thoughts. I just knew that she didn't want me to tell Dad about her outburst and the way I had run away.

It seemed a long time ago now. I knew that if I had told my dad about everything, there would have been a row between them and I would have felt wretched and unhappy all over again.

"May I leave the table Mum?" I asked politely. Mum nodded and I ran to my carrier and plucked out Betsy.

"Look at my doll, Dad, she's got a new pink dress; Aunt B made it for me." I held her high up in my hand and I stroked the buttons, but then I frowned. My excitement mingled with the thoughts of Aunt B. With deep affection, I sighed; I realised I had to get on with the present and push the past behind me. I watched Dad as he sipped his mug of hot tea.

"Was there a raid last night, Dad?"

"Yes, love, near to the docks and town centre." His answer was muffled by the food in his mouth.

"We saw all the debris on our way home," Mum stated, then she turned to me, "Come on, Mary, it's bed for you. You've had a long day."

I realised I had a day that I would never forget. Worst of all was leaving Aunt B and best of all was seeing my dad once again; but I vowed to remember everything Aunt B had taught me. Mum had put a hot water bottle in my bed, 'to air the sheets', she said, even though it was a hot summer's night. When I was tucked up in my bed with Betsy, Dad came in the room.

"Are you glad to be home, Mary?" he whispered, smiling. I thought a moment, about the farm and Aunt B and then I looked into Dad's laughing, twinkling eyes.

"Yes," I sighed. Then his face turned serious

"Mary, if you hear a siren, it means there's a raid and we will have to go to the shelter. Don't be afraid, your mum will look after you."

I felt excited, "I'm not frightened, Dad."

He smiled and whispered as he pecked my cheek, "Night, night little bird, I'm glad you're home, love."

As I lay there, I started to think of the last twenty four hours, but sleep overtook my thoughts.

I awoke early and, wearing only my nightie, I ran downstairs. Dad was struggling into his overalls, but he gave me a glass of milk and some toast. I shivered.

"Here put this round you." And he put his old grey cardigan around my shoulders, tying the long sleeves in a loose knot across my chest.

"I feel much more awake after having had no raid last night! I had a good night's sleep!" he smiled.

"Mary, your mum is still in bed, I've taken her some tea." He then looked serious. "She gets angry sometimes, love. It's just her way, you know."

I didn't know exactly what Dad meant, but I was finding out. Yesterday, she was quiet and calm, but my mind raced to the day before, when I saw her in a different light and how she caused Aunt B and me such pain. Dad waved to me.

"See you tonight, Mary, be good," and he walked through to the back yard to get his bike.

As I sat at the table, I talked to Betsy, "My tooth's loose," and I waggled my front milk tooth. It felt as if it were hanging by a thread. Mum came into the living room, yawning, rubbing her eyes.

"I thought you would still be in bed, Mary," she said sleepily. Then she pointed at my breakfast and stared at all my left over crusts. I looked up at her.

"I don't like crusts, Mam."

"Crusts are good for your teeth," she growled. "You're not going out to play until you have eaten them."

I sat and stared at the hard, dry bread, while Mum poured out another cup of tea for herself. She put her elbows on the table and watched me. I gingerly bit into the crust and chewed, looking forlorn.

"I've eaten some, Mam."

"You eat it all, or you'll stay here till dinner time!" she snapped. I frowned, the bread was so hard and my tooth hurt. Then Mum walked into the scullery to put more water in the kettle. I took advantage of her flight and I grabbed a handful of crusts and stuffed them into Dad's cardigan pocket. When she came back into the room, I chewed at another piece of crust, but each time she looked away, I proceeded to fill my pocket. I stared at the last crust on my plate and looked sheepishly at Mum. She sighed and took the plate away from me.

"I'll give that bit to the birds." I leaned back in my chair and giggled as Mum shouted from the yard.

"When I've washed up, Mary, I need to go on the avenue to get some groceries."

After I had washed my face and gently cleaned my teeth, Mum helped me put on my sandshoes. She tried to show me how to do up a bow with the laces, but I found it a complicated procedure. It was a fine sunny morning; the avenue looked cleaner than yesterday. People seemed to be in high spirits, more alert after a night of uninterrupted sleep. Mum passed the time of day with one or two neighbours. Everyone remarked about my reappearance and Mum politely lied, saying I couldn't settle and that I wanted to come home. She ignored my protests as I pulled on her arm. We stood and queued at Jackson's, the local grocery shop, for a loaf of bread and queued again at Home & Colonial near the corner of Alexander Road. I liked this shop, all the counters were made of grey speckled marble. There was a giant bacon-slicer and the grocer, in his blue apron, would turn a big brass handle and a huge saw would start to rotate. Sugar was weighed by the pound in dark blue, coarse paper bags and you could buy flour by the stone. The smell of tea and coffee gave the shop a delicate aroma, but Mum bought cocoa for me - it was my favourite drink. Although this shop seemed an 'Aladdin's cave' of goodies, it was not so. Rationing had been introduced and only a small amount would reach our basket. Tea was down to 2 ounces per person, per week and sugar, 8 ounces per person, per week. Because so many hens had been slaughtered, there was a scarcity of eggs, making them a rare commodity. In place of eggs, we were allowed egg powder: one packet per month. The butter, lard, and margarine ration added up to only 8 ounces per week and only 2 ounces of cheese, so it didn't take long to buy one's weekly ration, but it took time to queue for it. One shilling and two pence would buy one's weekly meat ration. Mum would buy lots of vegetables and pile them on our plates to make a wholesome meal. There was a thriving black market and, although it was against the law, my father would bring home a joint of meat which he had purchased underhandedly from some stranger at the docks. It would last us the week and we had no fridge or freezer. The meat would be eked out over the days and we didn't seem to suffer from food poisoning. Although everything was rationed, I seemed to be always eating when I was at the farm, food was so plentiful there. The stark reality hit home as I watched Mum's weary expression, as she juggled with her coupons in the ration book. Mum gave me the string bag to carry and in it was a four pence, half penny, two pound loaf, a two ounce block of cheese and a packet of cocoa.

"Hello, Mary." It was Mrs Dunne. She lived in the next terrace to ours - 'Sevendale' - and she always talked to me.

"Have you come back to see us then?" she asked.

"Yes, will we get a raid tonight?" I asked excitedly.

"Nay, love, I hope not," she sighed. "I see you're helping your Mum do the shopping."

Mum nodded and smiled. Mrs Dunne produced an 'Arrowroot' biscuit from her bag.

"Here you are, dear." She was a nice old lady. When we reached home, my mum let me play. I looked once more into my new-found toy box. I remembered that the crusts from my toast were still in my dad's cardigan pocket, so when Mum was out of the room, I carefully emptied the pockets inside out over my toy box; no one would ever find them there.

Chapter 7
'My First Air Raid'

As I sorted through my toys, I kept nudging my tooth with my tongue. The tooth could now be pushed backwards and forwards, I just needed to be brave and pull on it. I picked up my favourite story book, Brer Rabbit, and stared at the pictures.

With my index finger and thumb, I pulled and I pulled at my tooth. I could hear the tiny threads of root as they broke away. Finally, my tooth came away in my hand. It hadn't hurt me after all, but it left a salty taste in my mouth. I went to the sink and spat out the congealed blood and after a drink of water, I was fine. I proudly went to Mum; she was on her knees with a hand brush and shovel.

"Look, Mam, my tooth's come out." I pushed my tongue into the crevice where my tooth had once been.

Mum rubbed her hands on her thighs. "Oh dear, never mind. Put it under the door mat and the fairies might come."

I frowned; under the door mat seemed a funny place to put a tooth, but I did as I was told all the same. The next morning I lifted up the corner of the matting. My tooth was gone and in its place was a silver sixpence. When Dad arrived home that evening, I showed him my sixpence from the fairies. Dad laughed out loud.

"How would you like one of these sixpences every week, Mary?"

"Yes please," I grinned, showing the space where my tooth used to be.

Dad rubbed his chin thoughtfully, "You will have to earn it, Mary. I will think of something for you to do."

I showed Dad my drawings and he was quite impressed.

"She takes after you, Jack," Mum would say. Dad's real work was sign writing; he told me that he had designed and painted some of the big names on the stores in Hull, such as Hammonds, Thornton Varley's and Bladon's. He was very talented. He encouraged me to draw and crayon and this I loved to do.

If Mum wasn't cleaning, she would be darning socks or mending our clothes; even clothing was rationed. There were advertisements in the newspapers and huge hoardings showing the comic-like character of the 'Squander Bug', pressing the public to economise. We never threw anything away. Clothing was plentiful, but we didn't have the resources to purchase some items. Paper was scarce too; we never threw our papers away. Dad soon decided what I was to do for my pocket money. With our newspaper, I would cut it into small squares. Mum would pierce a hole in the corner with a darning needle and thread through a string and hang it in the lavatory in the yard. I would also fold paper into strips, to be used as tapers, instead of matches, for the coal fire. Mum placed them in a small blue vase on the mantelpiece. Each night, when Dad went out, he used to wear a khaki uniform and a tin hat. I am not sure what he did, but he remarked that he was helping the war effort.

We had four days without a raid and I was beginning to wonder what all the fuss was about. It was now August and Mum said that I would be starting school in September. I was looking forward to this; it would be another adventure for me. I still hadn't heard the sirens and like me, Mum and Dad were becoming apprehensive; the waiting wasn't to be long.

I went to bed about nine o'clock because Mum had let me finish off my drawing and Dad had let me use old watercolour paints. I had painted a picture of the farm and stood Auntie B in the centre. Dad liked it and gave it pride of place on the alcove, near the fireplace in the living room.

That night, I fell into a deep sleep, only to be awakened by Mum shaking me.

"Wake up, Mary, there's a raid."

I soon realised I wasn't dreaming. Quickly, I pulled on my clothes, as Mum was panicking and nudging me.

"Hurry, we must get to the shelter." Her voice was sharp and high pitched; I could see that she was in that mode of hysteria I had seen back at the farm. I did as I was told, but I grabbed Betsy as I flew out of the room. I almost fell in the darkness, as Mum dragged me to the front door. The sounds that met my ears were voices and the droning moan of the siren, a sound with which I was to become all too familiar. It was very dark and, with other neighbours, we held hands, as we filed down the terrace towards the brick shelter. Suddenly, there was a sound like thunder. A spasm of stars crackled overhead in the pitch-black of the sky. I wanted to watch, but Mam lifted up the sacking and dragged me through the opening of the brick shelter. It smelt musty, like old damp clothes. Mum found a seat and laid a small woollen cover over it, so we didn't feel the bare boards against our bottoms. Mrs Dunne was sat beside us, she was shining a torch in my face.

"Don't be afraid, love. You'll be alright," she whispered. I felt that she was saying that to cover her own fear, because I didn't feel afraid at all, just full of wonder.

We settled down and waited; it sounded like a storm outside. I stared all around me. From the ceiling protruded a grubby sixty-watt bulb; it gave little light and caused heavy shadows to appear. I saw one of my friends who lived near Mrs Dunne, her name was Beryl.

"It's like thunder, isn't it?" I shouted excitedly. She just sat there, looking afraid, her mum caressing her. My mum never put her arms around me like that.

Mrs Dunne gestured to us both and gave us a 'Nice' biscuit. We sat still, all of us preoccupied with daunting thoughts. One or two women were knitting, unconcerned and a couple of old men were playing drafts in the corner. The strip of old sacking over the doorway was suddenly pulled up and an Air Raid Precautions warden peeped in.

"Everyone all right?" the ARP warden shouted.

"Of course we are. Many bombs?" one of the old men retorted.

The warden clicked his tongue, "Aye, at the docks. East Hull, I think. It's gonna to be a long night," he sighed and after a second he disappeared.

I felt wide awake and stared around me. I realised Dad wasn't there.

"Mam, where's Dad?" I asked.

"He's on duty," she snapped, obviously anxious, "Close your eyes and try to get some sleep, Mary."

How could I sleep with all this drumming and whistling around? Mrs Dunne looked thoughtful as she nibbled a second biscuit.

"You know, I might have been better off under my stairs."

"Oh you're much safer in here, love," an old man answered, smiling.

I managed to get snatches of sleep between low-pitched voices and distant crackling of thunder.

"It does sound way off, tonight!" Beryl's mother stated.

"But someone's in trouble," sighed Mrs Dunne.

We sat in the shelter for about five hours then, finally, the all clear sounded. We all stretched our stiffened limbs as we filed out of the shelter. I yawned and took a deep breath, only to be choked by smoggy morning air. Mum took me straight to bed and I fell asleep as soon as my head touched the pillow. It was to be the first of many such nights.

Dad told me that he was in the Home Guard and, after working all day, he would go on duty, leaving Mum and I alone every evening. I don't know when or how he managed to get any sleep, but he seemed to cope.

In September, Mum walked with me to Newland Avenue Primary School. She thought my first day would have been traumatic, but I must have been the exception to the rule. I loved it and I watched, unconcerned, as the other children cried and longed for their mothers. I cheekily chatted to Miss Barker, the teacher. I was growing quite used to strangers. She let me draw, crayon and play with the plasticine. I never wanted to go home, but I was still a shy child and my only real friend seemed to be Beryl.

Mum was acting strangely, filling the house with packing cases and, when I came home from school, she would shut the lids quickly, as if she had something to hide; she was very preoccupied. While most mums were cooking and cleaning, my mum had other ideas.

It was now October and the nights were becoming colder and darker. Mum would sit, night after night, constantly sewing garments, some of which I had never seen before.

I would sit and draw by the open fire and listen to 'The Tommy Handley Show'; it was always full of laughter. There was a cosy feeling inside me as I relaxed. The tall standard lamp would be lit and a shaft of mellow light would fall across the room, cocooning our presence. One evening, as Dad was getting ready for duty, Mum leaned back from her sewing and smiled, "Jack, I've got it; the shop. And it's a small rent too." She looked excited.

Dad looked concerned.

"If that's what you want, Eth, but what about Mary?"

Mum stared down at her sewing, "Oh, she'll be alright."

Those words brought a cold shiver down my spine. I remembered the last time Mum had uttered those words in Paragon Station and I stared at Mum questioningly. Mum laid her sewing on her knees and looked towards me.

"I've rented a little shop, Mary, down Alexandra Road."

"But what are you going to sell, Mam?"

"Second-hand clothes of course," she snapped.

She had seen there was a market to be had, because of the clothes rationing. Dad painted the outside of the shop dark green. I had my doubts as to where he had purchased the paint, because the daubs on his white working overalls were the same colour. He designed posters and stuck them on the windows, they read: 'MRS THOMPSON, high class wardrobe dealer'. Inside was an old chest of drawers and Dad had fixed a metal rail along one side of the wall, on which hung a mixture of ladies' and men's clothing and in a corner, on a small table, was a washing basket full of baby clothes. There was even a wooden cash till. Dad also rigged up a dividing curtain, so Mum had a small private area where she could have a cup of tea. It was quite exciting really and I warmed to the fact of my mum having her own shop and I wanted to help. I had to attend school, but Mum promised I could help out on a Saturday. Each morning, if we hadn't had a raid the night before, Mum would accompany me to school, she would then go on to her shop. At lunch time, she would meet me and buy two pennies' worth of chips for my dinner. I liked sitting behind the curtain eating my chips, while Mum served customers; the smell of vinegar didn't deter them! There was one thing I wasn't too pleased about: Mum had found a second hand gabardine, she said it was just my size. She rolled up the sleeves and took up the hem, said I would grow into it, but I felt like I was wearing Dad's overcoat!

    The business was doing well. Mum was kept busy and some of the customers became friends; many had riveting tales to tell. Some people would confide in Mum, treating her like an agony aunt, though I felt that she was the last person on earth to whom I would tell my troubles. She showed a more caring attitude when she was behind her counter and she enjoyed her new role of shopkeeper. A few weeks before Christmas, I helped Mum put up paper chains to give the shop a jolly atmosphere. Lots of people were buying clothing for the Christmas break and in between raids, everyone tried to be cheerful. We had spent many nights in the shelter, but at least the raids were away from the Newland Avenue area, though eastern parts of Hull were targeted, so Christmas Day was spent with weary hearts. In my stocking I found an apple, a box of paints, a comic and a magic painting book. That was great fun. I just had to apply water with my brush and, as if by magic, different colours appeared. As an extra treat, I found a packet of Maltesers.

The new year of 1941 began quietly, a few nights without a raid; the weather was fine, but cold. Dad was in the back yard, cleaning his bike. I stood in the doorway, watching.

"What do you think?" he asked, tapping a small saddle on the crossbar. "Shall we go for a ride to see Grandma?"

I took a deep intake of breath with excitement.

Chapter 8
'Grandma Thompson'

After dinner we set off down the road. I felt that I was flying, sitting on the cross bar as Dad propelled us along. The air was cold, but I was warm in my pixie hood and mittens. I must have looked a sight: my hands firmly clutching the handlebars and my small legs spread-eagled so as not to get in the way of Dad's thighs as he peddled along.

Grandma's house was down Finsbury Street, off Fountain Road, which was off Beverley Road. To get onto Beverley Road, Dad cut through Pearson Park, then we came to Cave Street, but we had to walk a little of the way down the street because there had been some bombing. Large bricks and rubble were strewn along the tarmac and all down one side of the street was a row of only four houses with just their gable ends standing, their inside walls showing different colours of wallpaper patterns and stippling white wash. All that remained of people's homes, like sentries in the wind. That was my first real shock at the devastation, seeing what damage the bombs could really do, but apart from the bumpy ride along the cobblestones off Fountain Road, we arrived safely.

Grandma's house was quite small: 1, Bohemia Terrace, Finsbury Street. The staircase came into the living room via a slanted pine door. A large 'Yorkist' range dominated the room; it had two large ovens, a place to store fire wood and a deep grate with a welcoming fire. The smell of fresh bread enveloped us as we walked into the kitchen. It was hard to believe there was a war on. The table was laden with tarts, scones and fruit pies and, at the end of it, stood my grandma. Dad grinned.

"Hello, Mum. Mary's back from Selby. Thought we would come and see you; I've put a saddle on my old bike. It's a good job she's a little bird," he laughed.

"Why it's grand to see you, love," she laughed, as she pecked my cheek.

I thought this grandma was beautiful and, in a strange way, a little like Auntie B. Her hair was drawn back off her rather big face. She had very rosy cheeks which were emphasised by her almost white hair. She had a big bosom; I called it cuddly. She was forever baking and she spoke with a funny accent too. She would call me 'bain', 'lassie' and sometimes 'pet', like Auntie B used to do. She had fat arms, with sleeves always rolled up to her elbows. Grandma would always save a tiny amount of pastry for me and I had my own small rolling pin. Oh, how I enjoyed being in that warm cosy kitchen, helping my grandma and I remembered the time I had helped Aunt B in the same way. Grandma Thompson had six sons and daughters, so I had lots of aunts and uncles. I think they were all married and away from home, but Grandma couldn't get out of the habit of cooking for a large family. Seeing all this food gave me an appetite, but Grandma put her fat, floury fingers firmly on my shoulders:

"Wait while the baking is finished lass."

My granddad was at work; he was the head chef at the Kingston General Hospital on Beverley Road. Although they were both very happy, there was a sort of rivalry between them regarding the baking and cooking. My dad set about chopping wood and bringing in coal for the fire. It was nearly teatime and my mouth was watering.

Grandma gave a big sigh at last, "Well, that's it for today, lass." She stood in front of the stove, rubbing her hands together on her white apron, "I could do with a drink," and she reached to the top of the high mantelpiece and lifted down a tall white jug. "Here put your coat on and go and get my stout, lass."

As I slid into my gabardine, I was thinking of Mrs King's, the local corner shop. I hurried; I loved going there. I would stand and stare at all the tall jars of boiled sweets and sniff the aroma of cider, chocolate and liquorice. The shop was quite full, so I stood behind the other customers and waited, my jug in one hand, my pennies in the other. Mr King, the shopkeeper, was a small, bald-headed man with a jolly manner. He left his other customers and peered down at me.

"Is that little Mary I see? I know, some stout for your gran, eh, love?"

"Yes please," I whispered and I passed the large jug over the hinged counter. I watched and slowly, as if by magic, he drew on a pump and the brown frothy liquid flowed, filling up Grandma's jug. He took a large checked tea towel and wiped the outside and then pushed the jug slowly towards me. I passed him my pennies along the worn counter.

"Don't drop it, mind," he added and I was about to leave when he shouted, "'ere don't forget your sweetie." He held out a toffee, wrapped in red cellophane paper.

"Thanks," I whispered, grinning from ear to ear.

I walked very slowly, as the jug was now quite heavy and I didn't want to spill Grandma's stout. I felt happy as I looked at my wonderful toffee; I would save it for after.

Back at Grandmas, I had a beaker of steaming cocoa. Grandma sat on the Chippendale chair by the fire; she rubbed the corner of her pinafore across her forehead. She poured her stout into a large mug and took a long gulp and smiled as she rubbed the back of her hand across her mouth. I was staring at the 2lb glass jam jar in front of me, full to the brim with pork dripping and aspic jelly. I could feel my mouth watering. Grandma laughed as she handed me dripping sandwiches. I grabbed at the thick slices of bread and bit into my sandwich hastily; the taste was heaven. Grandma took a bite of a tart and turned to me.

"Steady, you're eating like a tramp."

Dad smiled as he looked at my worried face.

"A tramp eats like you or I, love," then he laughed.

Granddad came in from his day in the hospital kitchens. "Mary, love," he beamed.

I watched him as he walked into the kitchen. He pulled my grandma towards him and kissed her fondly on the lips. He gave her his jacket. He was wearing a waistcoat, from the top pocket hung a gold fob chain. His eyes were brown and bright, like my dad's, only his hair was greying and he needed a shave. I noticed his shirt sleeves were rolled up too, like Grandma's.

Grandma let him have his chair by the warm fire. His eyes scanned the table.

"I see you've been baking again, Jane," he said, smiling, shaking his head in disbelief at the volume of food in front of him. Then he took a tin from the mantelpiece and reached for his pipe out of the rack. After he had filled his pipe, he plunged a taper into the fire and proceeded to light it and with that, clouds of white smoke puffed towards the ceiling. As he laid his head back, he spoke to Grandma: "Jane, tek ma boots off, lass, will yer?"

She immediately dropped to her knees to do her husband's bidding. Grandma could never do enough for Granddad; they were both so loving and depended solely upon one another. Though life was hard, it made them strong and created a bond of love between them.

As Dad brought in the firewood, he turned to his dad.
"Any luck with the horses, Dad?"
Granddad studied his 'Sporting Pink' at length.
"Not a one," he sighed, as he licked his blue lead pencil.

My granddad liked his little bet on the horses, it was his only vice. With the odd sixpence, he would back the one hundred to one choice, dreaming, like everyone does, of winning big.

He turned to Grandma, "Ma, you'll 'ave to tek me suit back on Monday."

He spoke broad Yorkshire dialect. I had to listen carefully to get the gist of his speech. After a few seconds, I realised he was referring to the pawnshop. Grandma would pawn his best Sunday suit during the week, pledging it and reclaiming it on a Saturday morning, before church service on a Sunday. And I think that Granddad's old fob chain and watch weren't always in his waist coat pocket! After I had eaten, Granddad gave me my old drawing book. I scrambled onto the horsehair settee and happily set about my sketching, as I sucked on my toffee. It was growing dark, so Granddad decided to light the mantle. They didn't have electricity, like our house. Granddad stood on a small stool and reached towards a fitting in the centre of the ceiling and, with a taper, he lit the delicate bulb. It was a very dull light, but after a few minutes the room seemed to become brighter. It was either that or we became used to the dimness. Grandma offered me another tart, but I declined.

"What did I tell you, she eats like a bird, that one," Dad remarked, tucking into his third sandwich.

Granddad fluffed up a cushion and beckoned me to sit by him. I slid my hand along the shining brass top of the fireguard as it glistened from the flames. I sat on the cushion and looked at the room. There was the crackle of the fire, the smell of the baking and the wireless droning in the background. Grandma sat with her stout, contentedly staring into the flames, occasionally poking at the embers and Granddad continued to read his evening paper; the warmth of the room washed over me. Only in this house, did I feel absolutely relaxed. If there was a heaven, I would wish it to be here. The room glowed with tranquillity. Both Gran and Granddad had time to stop and listen to the chatter of a mischievous grandchild, but it didn't last forever. Soon it was time for us to go home.

As we were about to go, I heard Dad's voice.

"Oh no, my back light is broken."

The red glass from his back lamp was in splinters along the garden path, but the actual bulb still worked. I frowned, and then I remembered,

"I know what to do, Dad," I said, excitedly. I ran to the old sofa, pushed my hand under the seat, and retrieved the red cellophane paper from my sweet. I spread it out on the kitchen table and smoothed it with my fingers.

"Look, Dad, you can use this," and I held out the red paper.

Dad laid the paper between the rim and the bulb. There was just enough and it shone red.

He turned and looked my way, "You're a wise little bird, you are! Clever girl."

I felt very proud, as everyone looked at me, smiling. I kissed them both goodbye and Granddad felt in his breast pocket.

"Don't spend it till next week, mind," and he gave me a three penny bit piece.

"Take care now," Grandma pushed a paper bag full of tarts in my hands.

We hugged and said our goodbyes.

Grandma shouted, "Away, lass, away," and in the dusky evening, we made our way back home.

We were into the middle of January 1941, the weather was cold, but we had no snow. I wrote about my Grandma Thompson in my diary, it was a notebook really, but I felt that it was like a real diary. Mum continued to open her shop and we muddled through each and every day.

One Sunday, Dad took me to Pearson Park, off Princes Avenue, where we had taken the short cut to my grandma's house. It was a small park and as we walked through the long winding path of the entrance, I noticed the swings to my right. I leapt gleefully onto a swing and Dad pushed me as high as the sky. I even went on the seesaw. I sat astride one end and Dad pressed down on the other, but my favourite ride was the hobby horse. It was an oblong structure on giant springs with about four padded saddles along the top.

When I sat on this, I felt that I was riding a bucking bronco. The park seemed very quiet, well, it was a cold morning. Only two or three other children seemed to be running around, enjoying the freedom. We then walked further into the park and to my right again, was a wondrous pond, edged with large mossy stones. It glittered a little as a weak, watery sun filtered through dense clouds. In some spots, thin slithers of ice broke away as little drunken ducks scrambled for a footing on its surface. As we walked on, Dad showed me the statue of Queen Victoria, who had opened the park many years ago and high above the statue, hovered the biggest silver balloon I had ever seen. Dad explained to me that most major towns and cities had barrage balloons in the sky to prevent the enemy from flying low over the city. The balloons were tethered to the ground by a series of steel ropes. It was an exciting spectacle; we watched it as it surged first to the right and then to the left, as the wind swirled around, lifting its huge bulk as it rebelled against the air. We walked back to the pond; the eider ducks huddled together on the bank for warmth and shelter, unaware of our intrusion into their park. The cold air danced before our breath and we felt elated and honoured at all this beauty; a mixed blessing in this war.

That night, when I wrote about the balloon, I drew a picture too. Our visits to the shelter were less frequent and there was hope in my heart as I climbed into bed each night. I would whisper to Betsy, "Maybe this war will end tonight, Betsy." I was optimistic, but little did I know then, that 1941 was to be the most dreadful year of the war.

Dad hadn't been home in two days and he looked very tired as he ate his tea, one evening. He picked up the evening Mail and, as usual, in between mouthfuls, he read snippets aloud. He then folded his paper and stared into the hearth, shaking his head. He plunged the poker deeply into the embers of the fire.

"What's it all about, Eth?"

Mum lifted her eyebrows and didn't answer.

I stared at them both. "What's wrong, Dad?"

Dad looked very despondent as he laid the poker along the grate and let out a deep sigh.

"Well, Mary, I work at Alexandra Dock. Myself and others have been working so hard to get ships seaworthy and both the vessels we worked on were sunk. There was a mine two nights ago; I didn't realise how badly they were damaged. Oh, I'm so saddened by it all. All that work in vain!"

I didn't answer; I didn't know what to say. How could I cheer Dad up? I went to him and held his hands.

"You've got me and Mum, Dad," I whispered.

He beamed at me, cupped his hands around my forehead and kissed it.

"What would I do without my little bird?"

Because we had been spared a raid, I had enjoyed a reasonable night's sleep. The weather was very cold, but we still hadn't had any snow, though this morning seemed exceptionally dark. I gasped as I stared out of my bedroom window. Just above the rooftops was the barrage balloon. I ran downstairs to tell Mum and we both rushed into the terrace. There was a lot of noise, like the rumble of thunder. The barrage balloon from Pearson Park had broken from its moorings and was heading our way. The heavy rumble was caused by all the steel ropes now dangling like feelers from a jellyfish, as it moved along Goddard Avenue. The ropes were breaking everything in their path: roofs, chimney stacks, telephone wires, walls and windows. Sparks hissed and crackled in the icy air, slates tumbled to the ground and great chimneys smashed to pieces as they thumped into the pavements. Everyone fled, for fear of falling debris. The noise filled our ears and the balloon seemed to fill the sky as it swished quickly past my house and onward towards Chanterlands Avenue, leaving utter chaos in its wake. I wanted to linger and watch it as it sped away, but Mum finally dragged me to school, but that day, all we talked about was the balloon and its antics.

Luckily our house wasn't damaged and I thought about the balloon's flight as it ventured on. Maybe it would be lost in the clouds, never to be seen again.

I was learning my times tables and every day we chanted: 'One two is two, two twos are four' and on and on, until we reached our twelve times table. My writing was improving and I think that because I wrote in my notebook, my grammar became more cultivated. It was incredible how we learned anything at all. Many times, I would be awoken by the teacher after I had fallen asleep at my desk. Probably the teachers were as tired as the children were, but they worked hard not to show it. The children were forever using their imaginations, playing different games in the playground: Hide and Seek, Hopscotch, Tig, Queenie, Jacks, Marbles and Cig Cards, but invariably, Beryl and I found a quiet corner where we could play our Cat's Cradle with our grubby loop of string.

Wherever I went, I always had to take my gas mask, but one or two of the children in my class neglected theirs, so every day the teacher would check that we hadn't forgotten them. One day, in assembly, Miss Barker told us that she would spring a surprise and pretend that there was a gas attack and see how quickly we could react to put on our gas masks. We just giggled and didn't take much notice. Later, we were reciting our tables when suddenly, the alarm sounded.

"Right, children, see how quickly you can put on your gas masks," our teacher shouted in a high- pitched tone. We fumbled with our string and boxes. One girl kicked her gas mask box and it landed across the room but finally, I managed to pull the thick rubber lining over my head. The strong smell of the rubber made me feel sick as I inhaled. The glass front panel steamed up as I groped to see the teacher, who, by now, looked very dismayed at our efforts. Our breathing was short and laboured, as the round filter at the front of our masks clicked up and then down, our faces clammy with hot breath. One misbehaved boy in the corner of the room nodded his head rapidly against the lid of his desk as he talked, like someone gagged. He mumbled, "'I don't like it m,m,m,m,m,misssss…"

The teacher pulled it off him and quietly laid it on the desk. Most of us sat, our arms folded, staring at each other and feeling silly. The teacher coughed and cleared her throat.

"That will be all for today children, you can take them off now, thank you. Mind you put them back in the boxes."

I just hoped that we would never have to wear them for real. That smell of strong rubber was so overpowering; surely nothing could smell worse than that!

Mum said that soon, she would take me to see my Grandma Emmitt, her mum. She lived in the country, in a village called Skidby. I hadn't seen her since I had been evacuated, so I was looking forward to the visit.

The days passed by and, finally, we had a little snow, but not nearly enough to make a snowman. I never felt the cold. There was one good point about my gabardine; I could wear lots of woollies underneath it. My black wellingtons were always beside the door; sometimes I would go to bed half dressed, the bedroom was so cold, but I would be prepared for a quick retreat to the shelter. We were now into March and the raids were becoming more frequent. Everyone seemed to be feeling edgy; sometimes we wearily trudged to the shelter, only to walk back home after a feverish few minutes. One evening, as Dad sat at the table, he was browsing through the evening newspaper.

"Listen to this, Eth. There have been parachute mines, damage to surrounding houses and causalities, some fatal. One blast was so bad, a man found himself stripped of his pyjamas, though he was unhurt!"

I think by this time, my dad had said that more than a hundred alerts had been sounded. The weather was extremely cold and the raids had started in earnest. It was Saturday morning; I felt quite alert. We had had a raid the night before, but it had happened between 8pm and 10pm, so I had had a reasonable night's sleep. Mum and I were eating breakfast and Dad had gone to work overtime at the docks. She looked happy today and, smiling, she announced that we were going to visit her mum, Grandma Emmitt. Mum was going to close her shop for the day.

Chapter 9
'Grandma Emmitt, Connie, and the Homecoming'

She dressed me in my great gabardine, pixie hood, and mittens. Mum wore some funny rubber boots what fitted over her shoes a black swagger coat and a paisley headscarf about her head. We took the '62' trolley bus to Botanic Crossings. We then walked to Spring Bank West, to the corner of Hymers Avenue. Here was yet another bus stop.

We stood there for an age, waiting, but I felt excited and I didn't feel the cold air at all. At last, an East Yorkshire bus appeared and we stepped aboard. I quickly found a seat by the window and was enthralled by the sound of the engine, so I hummed to its drumming and, as we drove along, I pretended I was in a car. Only rich people seemed to own cars. I had never ridden in a car, only my short trip in Tom's truck and it was rickety.

My grandma lived in a small cottage in Skidby; it consisted of about four rooms. One room had a pine fireplace, a large, worn, drop-end sofa; a clip rug lay next to the red hearth. A thin clothesline hung under the mantelpiece and steam clouded the air, as damp tea towels hung only feet away from the naked flames. There was always a welcoming fire and I would sit on the boxed ends of the brass curb that surrounded it. I would fantasise as I watched the sparks and flames lick the chimney. I don't ever remember a fireguard.

The other room was floored in grey paving stones, obviously the kitchen. In it, were a white Belfast sink, an old grey marble-effect cooker, a small pine table and a towering dresser, which filled the room. It was laden with many pots of all shapes and all kinds and many were quite dusty. The kitchen seemed very cramped and the size of the garden, compared with the size of the house, was very large. I think that the cottage was very old indeed. My grandma was a tall, slim lady with steel grey hair; it was thick, short and in an

'Eton Crop' style. She had delicate features and outstanding green eyes, like my mum's, but she seemed calmer, more serene. She stood in the doorway, rubbing her hands on her check apron.

"Well, now," she beamed, as I ran to her, "I hardly recognise you, Mary, you have grown so much." She gave me a hug and ushered us inside. "Come and get warm."

Inside, my Auntie Enid was there, sitting by the fire, reading a magazine.

"There's baby Mary," Aunt Enid shouted.

"Not a baby anymore," Mum sighed.

Aunt Enid gave me a big grin, "Like some milk, Mary?"

She gave me a beaker; in it was goat's milk. I sipped it warily; it didn't taste like school milk! Grandma looked serious as she spoke to Mum.

"Have the raids been bad, Ethel?"

"They are becoming more frequent, Mother," Mum replied.

"Can we stay, Mam?" I interrupted eagerly.

"Of course you can," Grandma replied without hesitation.

Grandma would let me sleep on the old drop-end settee, which was more fun than a real bed.

Grandma smiled, "Would you like to go in the garden, Mary, Granddad is feeding the goat?" Mum fussed around me and fastened up my coat again.

There was snow everywhere, but it was slushy. I could see Granddad in the distance, digging. He was a big man; I was always a little afraid of him. His complexion was ruddy and he wore thick bottle-bottomed glasses; his sight was quite bad, I felt sure that he couldn't see through them. I don't recall what his hair was like. He always wore a battered brown cap and he had an old, holey, green jumper over his waistcoat and he wore tarry, green, corduroy trousers. On his feet were big black boots; I'll swear that he went to bed in them. He blew on his hands and rubbed them together; his voice was deep and loud.

"Mary, you're a stranger, love," and he held out his strong hand to me.

"I didn't know you had a nanny goat, Granddad," I smiled.

He beckoned to me. "Come and say hello to her, if you like?"

The nanny goat with dense, matted hair, was quite small. She was supposed to be white, but she was very dirty. She ignored my presence, as she pulled on the grass under the thin layer of snow. Granddad gave me a little shovel and I helped him for a while, then the snowflakes started to fall, hesitating before touching the ground, lifted by the strong wind. As we went inside, the heat caught at our breath as we entered the cosy kitchen. After I had taken off my wet clothes, Grandma gave me a hot cup of cocoa. She handed me my drawing book and pencil and I sat contented, listening to the crackle of the logs in the hearth. I had a wonderful, undisturbed sleep that night. It was such fun to curl up on the old settee and be swathed in Grandma's knitted covers.

I awoke to more snow and, after a hurried breakfast, I soon ran into the garden, all virgin white, until I alighted in my wellies! The goat didn't seem to mind the weather; she eyed me warily, before continuing to munch from her trough.

I decided to make a snowman, but there were only about two inches of snow. So, unperturbed, I retrieved snow from every available spot in the garden. The day was sunny, yet crisp and I patted and prodded at my little snowman and hunted around for stones for his features. I embedded a thin twig across the bottom of his ball-shaped head, giving him a large mouth and I laughed at the rather solemn stance before me, so engrossed was I.

Grandma shouted from the kitchen doorway, "Mary, dinner is ready." She gazed at my snowman. "He's a fine snowman, isn't he, dear?"

She hung all of my damp clothes over the clotheshorse by the fire and I watched as the steam wormed its way into the room.

"Grandma, do you have a name for the goat?" I asked earnestly.

"No, I don't think she has a name," she frowned.

"I shall call her Connie," I remarked quickly.

"That's a nice name, Mary, where did you get that from?"

"Oh, a cat I once knew," and I sighed as I stared into the flames and thought lovingly of Aunt B and the farm.

Grandma sat me on a cushion on a wooden stool and produced our dinner. Although they didn't have much money, my grandma gave us a meal fit for a king: meat, potatoes, gravy and, best of all, Yorkshire pudding; we even had jelly and custard for afters.

After I had eaten, I felt very full and contented. Grandma put a large dish full of peelings on the table.

"Here you are, Mary. You can go and feed the goat, er, Connie, I mean," she laughed.

I stared at the peelings, then frowned up at her. "Does Connie eat anything, Grandma?

"Yes. Anything. That is why she is fenced in. If she was wondering about, she would eat all our vegetables and that wouldn't do, would it?"

I nodded in agreement, as everyone seemed to be busy clearing the table. I dressed quickly and, as I speedily pushed my arm through the sleeve of my gabardine, I knocked the newspaper onto the floor. As I picked it up, I thought of Connie. I trudged down the garden path; the wind had now subsided and everything was still and quiet. Connie eyed me with a slanted grin. I leaned over the little fence.

"Here you are, Connie. That's your name now," I smiled.

She devoured the peelings in two gulps. Then I pulled out the newspaper from under my gabardine and whispered, "I bet you can't eat this." I opened 'The News of the World', folded it into strips and tapped her gently on the nose. She tossed her head and proceeded to chew relentlessly through the whole issue. I stood there, my mouth wide open, thinking how tasteless all the news must have been. When she had eaten the last strip of the tabloid, she grunted and continued to drink her water trough dry.

"You are so funny!" I laughed.

When I went back to the house, Mum and Grandma were having a cup of tea. My aunt Enid looked away from her magazine.

"Shall I show you how to make some dancing girls, Mary?" She tore out a page from an old magazine. She cut a page into a strip, folded it over about two inches and then folded it over and over, until she had a long narrow strip. She cut out a shape on one side of the fold and when she unwound the paper, there was a row of ballerinas. It seemed so easy, but my efforts were undeniably shapeless! I was busy concentrating, when Granddad entered the room. He looked towards Grandma.

"Ma, where's my paper?"

As he hovered in the doorway, he seemed to fill it. I stared up at him and swallowed. I could taste my dinner in the back of my throat and my eyes dropped to the kitchen floor. I knew I had been naughty, but I daren't tell him. I treated Connie with much more respect from that moment on.

Soon it was time to say goodbye. I left Granddad still searching for his Sunday paper. Grandma gave me a goody bag full of nice things to eat: jelly babies and some flapjack she had made. She had also knitted me a small bag for my hankie for school. Best of all, she gave me all her E coupons for extra sweet ration. The weather stayed fine, but the snow was beginning to glisten; obviously, it was freezing again.

When we arrived on Newland Avenue, we were met by lots of policemen. As we started to walk down our street, I clutched at my small bag. A policeman came towards us. I could see fire engines and ambulances; lots of people rushing about, wardens comforting them. Around us, that same stale smell of smoke hovered. I strained my eyes as I looked for our terrace. I felt Mum's grip on my hand tighten. Her face was deathly white and I noticed how much she looked like her mum, as she stared, wide-eyed, towards our house. I stared up at her, but she pulled on my arm to stop my glance. She seemed to find it so hard to show any physical emotion.

The policeman gazed at us and held out his arms.

"Sorry, love, you can't go down there."

I could hear a crack in Mum's voice.

"But we live down here," she protested.

The policeman looked a little puzzled, his hand scratching his chin. "But how come you're not?"

Mum butted in. "We've been away for the weekend, staying with my mother. Has there been a bomb?"

He answered with a question. "Oh,'" he sighed, "what are your names?"

"Thompson, Mrs Thompson," Mum replied, now getting impatient, "We live down Alandale."

The policeman sighed, "Well, that's alright then. You see, Mrs Thompson, they are still digging."

"Digging?" Mum repeated.

"Yes, they're looking for…," he cleared his throat, "…er," he put the back of his hand to his mouth as he looked in my direction, "I'm afraid… er…, I'm afraid Sevendale had a direct hit and that's all I can tell you at the moment."

There was a silence between them, as they stared into each other's eyes. Mum was breathing very quickly, the pitch of her voice becoming higher.

"Have you seen my husband?" Her voice was now a screech. I saw tears well up in her eyes and I smiled to myself thinking, 'She does love him.'

The policeman shrugged his shoulders, but he was sympathetic and he told us we could go home and he hoped that everything would be alright.

The terrace which had been bombed was next to ours. I was thinking of my friend, Beryl, who lived there and Mrs Dunne. As Mum marched me up the street, fine hail stung our faces and the ground beneath our feet glistened in between smudges of ash, shrapnel, and debris. Mum was pulling on my arm erratically, all the while muttering: "Oh, God, what will our house be like? Come on, come on, Mary."

She was almost running; she was always in a hurry. We reached Alandale and beyond, where the next terrace had stood, lay a great space, rubble everywhere and one gable end leaned against the sky, as the ground beneath seemed to ferment. Weary workmen, standing in a long chain, were sifting through the rubble with their bare hands. We stood there, watching. I rubbed at my smarting eyes.

"Are they searching for bodies, Mam?" I whispered.

Without hesitating, she nodded her head.

"Yes, Mary, they are."

We turned away, feeling very sad for all the people around us. All the houses down our terrace had had their windows badly cracked or blown out and number six was no exception. We walked in to find chaos, as broken glass and crockery crunched beneath our feet. Plaster hung from the walls and huge cracks had appeared across the ceilings; dust coated everything. Mum put her hands to her mouth, gasping in sheer horror. For once, I was very quiet; I had nothing to say. I didn't like this part of the adventure. I bit my lip, as I wondered where my dad was.

I was looking at Mum all the time. Mum suddenly flopped on the fireside chair, scattering the fine powdery dust as she did so. She held her head in her hands and gave an exhausted sigh.

"Oh dear, I don't know where to start and I wonder who's missing?"

I picked up Betsy from the living room floor; she was still in one piece and I tapped her body to shake off the dust. I held her close, but all the while I was wondering about my dad.

A huge crack descended from the corner of the living room ceiling, spreading like a feeler towards the centre light fitting, flakes of whitewash coated everything. Mum took off her coat and started to clear up the mess. I heard her say to herself, 'I must keep busy! Jack can't come home to this!"

While she was busy, I sneaked out through the front door. As I walked down the terrace, I saw some of my school friends. They were pleased to see me safe, because I hadn't been in the shelter that night. Then I caught site of Beryl. I gasped; I was so happy to see that she was all right. She told me that she was with her mum in the shelter when the bomb dropped. She said that she had been so frightened and the bang had been so loud, she still couldn't hear properly. The loud noise had affected her ears, but a doctor had said that she would regain her hearing in a day or two. She was rubbing her tired, sore eyes after much crying. I felt so sad at that moment, she looked so dejected. She ran up to me and we hugged one another.

"I've lost my house," she whispered. We cried together; she didn't mention her mum, but kept saying she had lost all her dolls.

"All my toys," she moaned.

I stared at her grimy features, she looked so weary. She looked into my eyes and in between her sobs, she blurted out, "And they're looking for Mrs Dunne."

I took a deep breath and tried to change the subject.

"Here, have a jelly baby," and I offered her my small bag. She smiled at last.

We stood at the end of Alandale and stared around us. Dust hovered, as a large lorry drove forwards and backwards, its wheels sliding on the glass-like ice, as the driver juxtaposed his position in line with the debris. At the back of the lorry was a huge yellow crane, hanging like a dormant spider. Such devastation - and down our avenue! I suddenly felt very cold and I visibly shivered.

I thought of how I would feel if I could not just run back home right this minute and sit on my little chair and read my favourite Brer Rabbit book, or find my drawing book, my pencil case; everything! I spoke very slowly, thinking hard, "You... er... you can have my doll if you like."

I stared at dear Betsy. I held her in both hands and reached out slowly to Beryl. I patted her skirt and dusted her down. "She's a bit dusty, but she's still alright and they call her Betsy."

Beryl's face beamed.

"Oh, can I?" she shouted with delight.

I blinked to try to stop my tears and I whispered, "And I hope Mrs Dunne is alright, and my dad, too."

I watched Beryl's face closely, as she fingered the tiny pearl buttons on Betsy's jacket.

When I went back home, the house smelt of carbolic and Mum was up to her elbows in suds, scrubbing at the kitchen linoleum, almost rubbing the check pattern away. She looked weary, as she wiped her dripping hand across her forehead to move her falling hair. She looked up at me.

"Your father should have been home ages ago!" Then she bit her lip, not wanting to alarm me.

"Where is he, Mam?" I asked earnestly.

"Oh, he'll be back soon," she answered quickly and she continued to scrub and ignored my presence.

I wandered out again.

As firemen collected their hoses and workmen continued to sift through the rubble, the grey slush was hardening. After I had stood for a while, I began to feel cold, so I ventured back home. This time I went down the back passage. Mum had left the back door open, maybe to let the dust settle. I ran past Mum and stood by the inviting fire. Mum was in still in shock and she was visibly angry.

"At last." Her voice was icy and it rang in my head. "It's about time. Where have you been? You could have helped me clean this mess!"

"So, what?" I retorted cheekily and within a second, a loud slap rang in my head. I dived under the table.

Mum was in one of her hysterical moods. She had been so different at Grandma's house. I knew that she was upset, but why was she always so angry? I wished at that moment that Dad would walk in. I felt my cheek, it was burning.

As I knelt under the table I felt safe, so I waited. A few minutes later, as if nothing had happened, Mum walked into the room and she told me to wash my hands. She had made some soup.

I tucked into mine; I was very hungry, but Mum just toyed with her spoon. She threw her head back and sighed.

"It's no good, I'm not hungry," she said, pushing her tureen away from her, "I'll warm it up later."

She just sat and stared at the tablecloth. When I had eaten, I thought it best if I cleared away the pots and as I did so, I noticed how clean and tidy the whole room seemed to be. My mum had worked magic after such chaos. I had taken it all for granted and been cheeky too.

Mum gradually became calmer.

"Come on, Mary, put your coat on and we'll see if we can find your dad."

I felt happy at this remark.

Mum wore her black swagger coat and her grey beret; she then wrapped her paisley scarf around her neck and pulled on a scarf ring for decoration.

Outside, there was the noise of motors and engines and there was now a crane in a precarious position. The engine laboured loudly, as it worked in unison with the workmen as they attached a cable around the remainder of the wall left standing. We stood at the end of our terrace and looked around. Mum frowned and put her fingers to her lips.

"I wonder which way?"

It was starting to get dark, but as I looked towards Newland Avenue, I caught sight of him. I easily recognised my dad and my body shook with delight.

'Dad! Dad! He's there, Mam, look!" I pointed to the other side of the road.

Walking towards us was a group of men, dishevelled, dirty and tired, their heads bowed, almost asleep on their feet. Amongst them was my dad. He stumbled as he walked along, his arms outstretched, his black hair strewn across his face like a man demented, his features grey and his big brown eyes glazed in tears. Sweat stains ran down his shirt from his racked, tired body. His broken voice began chanting.

"Eth, Eth. Thank God!" And I watched my dad reach out to my mum to embrace her. I watched her face, as she shied away from his dirty clothes as he hugged her, unaware of her abhorrence. He gave a quivering sigh and grabbed my hand.

"Mary!"

"Oh, Dad!" I cried. "We stayed at Grandma's, Dad."

"Oh, I'm so glad you're alright," he cried.

He kissed me hard on the cheek, but when he kissed Mum, she pulled away.

"You're all dirty, Jack," she snapped.

I stepped back and stared at both of them. How could she worry about the dirt? But that was my mother.

Dad gripped my hand tightly as we walked to our house. When he had taken off his wet jacket, he stood with his two fists leaning on the kitchen table and looked directly at Mum.

"If only you knew, Eth. We've been digging for bodies and searching everywhere. I thought that you and…" His voice weakened as he stared towards me.

He steadied himself, as tiredness overwhelmed him. He was exhausted, but he confronted her.

"Why, in God's name, didn't you tell me that you were going for the weekend? I've been out of my mind worrying."

"Didn't think," Mum snapped, shrugging her shoulders.

He snapped back, "Didn't think! That's you all over isn't it? You don't think of anyone but yourself, do yer?"

I sat in the corner of the room trying to read Brer Rabbit, but Mum and Dad were arguing again and I was beginning to feel sorry for Dad; did my mum love Dad at all?

When I was in bed that night, Dad gave me a goodnight kiss and when he hugged me, he seemed to hold me for ages. I had to pull away from him and there were tears in his eyes.

I lay awake for some time, thinking about Mum and Dad. I could hear voices, but they were talking quietly. I was thinking of the bomb, the casualties, Mrs Dunne and I wondered where she was and I could see Beryl's tearful face. I missed holding Betsy and I twisted the winceyette sheet in my fingers. Tomorrow, I would bring my old toy panda from my toy box for comfort.

Most of all, I kept thinking of my dad; he was actually crying for me and Mum. I stared into the shadowy darkness of my room. "Why must there be wars, it makes everyone so angry."

I missed Betsy, but I knew that Beryl would love her as I did.

Chapter 10
'Mrs Dunne and Dad'

Suddenly, everything around me was grey. Mrs Dunne stood before me with her hands outstretched; she held out a biscuit. I went towards her and we walked together hand-in-hand down our street. Before us lay a deep crater; we stood at the edge and peered down. Mrs Dunne threw her basket down into the deep hole and shouted, "Come, let's jump. Don't be afraid, you will fly."

As I leaned over the edge, her voice seemed to echo. Beryl was there, she pulled on my arm and we both leapt into the abyss. My body was falling.

"No, no, no…!" I shouted.

"Mary, come on," shouted Mrs Dunne, as she drifted down and down.

I screamed as I was falling deeper and deeper, "No, no…"

"Mary! Mary!" Dad was by my side, shouting my name, "You had a bad dream, love."

I rubbed my eyes and looked around me; most of my blankets were on the floor. My face was moist with salty tears.

"Please, I don't want to go with Mrs Dunne. I can't go back to sleep."

Dad frowned, "Here, sit up little bird and I'll make your bad dream go away."

He quickly lifted and fluffed-up my pillow and turned it over. I settled down once more and he looked into my eyes, "No more bad dreams; only happy ones," and he pecked my cheek affectionately. "God bless," he whispered, as he stepped out of the room.

We had had a night without a raid, but my night was racked with the thoughts and emotions of a mixed-up child.

The next morning, I walked to school with my friend Beryl. She and her mum were staying with a neighbour until they could find a new home. We watched, as other school friends retrieved bits of shrapnel embedded in icy puddles. The debris could be as far as a street away from its actual impact. The torrid smell of smoke and phosphorus never seemed to leave our nostrils.

At the end of Goddard Avenue, a police box stood. A crowd of mothers were straining to look at the casualty list which was regularly pinned upon the door. Beryl and I stood on tiptoes, but we still couldn't reach to see the names.

When we arrived at school, we had hymn singing and prayers. I kept my eyes open all the time; I couldn't stop thinking about Mrs Dunne. At playtime we were allowed outside because the weather was a little milder and the snow was turning to slush.

Beryl and I played a game with some other friends. The game was called: 'I Form a Statue'. One girl would hold the hand of another, spin her around whilst chanting the words: 'I form a statue, a pretty little statue; I form you' and then she would let her go and she would stand like a statue. This was done by each girl or boy in turn, then the spinner picked out the best and the whole performance started again.

It was one of many games of make-believe we played. All children needed so much to pretend, to dream and to mask their own reality from the deprivations of war. I found it hard to be a carefree child, but I had my vivid imagination, which helped.

My pretence helped me to muddle through everyday life. I don't know how the teachers coped each day. They shrouded out all the turmoil; they were pleasant and patient. And in a sad way, four, five and six year olds were quite old for their years. When one is a child, one always wishes to be older, but the war was to blame for a generation of old fashioned children; war babies were a breed of strong willed human beings.

Like many other children, I loved sweets. There was a treat Mum made up for me; I had a small Ovaltine tin and in it, was a teaspoonful of cocoa and a little sugar. I kept it inside my school desk. During lessons I would lift up the lid and dip in my moist index finger and lick my lips and my teacher never found out. At least we had good teeth; it was a small price to pay.

As I came out of school that day, my mum was at the school gate. She was wearing her blue paisley headscarf and, although her face looked pale, I could see she had dabbed her cheeks with rouge and her lips were smudged with lipstick. She was smiling; she didn't often do that. I ran up to kiss her, but she turned her head and I ended up kissing her powdered cheek As we walked home, I eyed her, my head on one side. I wondered why she wasn't at her shop; she didn't usually meet me from school. She was walking at a fast pace and chattering about shopping and housework; I couldn't seem to get a word in edgeways.

I finally blurted out, "Mam, I've done a picture for you."

In my sticky fingers I held out a sheet of grey recycled paper, on which I had drawn lots of people in coloured crayons. I proceeded to explain, "That's you, that's Dad and that's me and…"

"Yes, Mary," she snapped and she snatched the paper from my hands. She quickly stuffed it in her basket, without giving it a second glance. I gave a choked sigh. When we arrived home, Mum popped the kettle on the fire grate, she then came towards me.

"Mary, love," she whispered. She held both my hands and pulled me towards the sofa. I hadn't even taken off my gabardine.

"Sit down," she beckoned, "I've got something to tell you."

She faced me, her eyes blinking, forcing back her tears. "It's about the other night, love, when we had the raid. When we stayed at Grandma's house, I er…"

I stared wide-eyed into her eyes, waiting.

She put her hand to her face and sniffed, 'I… I… I've forgotten some shopping."

I crinkled up my nose; was that all she wanted to say? I didn't understand.

Mum cleared her throat, "Take this bag and this purse."

The purse contained one shilling, four large pennies and a halfpenny.

"Ask for a large loaf and two ounces of Spam; can you remember?"

"Yes, Mam," I answered, somewhat bemused.

As I walked down the avenue, I felt very mixed up. There was much activity, even though it was growing dark. I searched all the doorways and looked in all the shop windows; I was looking for Mrs Dunne. Some of my friends were playing marbles or hopscotch along the pavement, where the snow had melted. They were blowing warm breath through cupped hands. It was dusk and the sky was low with foreboding snow. The air was quite mild, but I felt cold.

Lingering inside me was a deep sadness, to think of my street, now so disfigured.

Many people walked about as if in a dream, staring into grey space.

I reached Jackson's shop to find a queue of people, which I duly joined. As I waited, I looked around me, but I couldn't see Mrs Dunne; she would probably be in the shop, buying her bread. Sometimes, I would help to carry her shopping. When she arrived at her terrace, she would fumble in her bag; she always had a biscuit for me. She was a tiny lady and she always wore a brightly coloured, brimmed hat and she smiled a lot. I couldn't see anything bright in the distance.

When it was my turn to be served, I had to stand on tiptoes to reach the marble-topped counter. I had to shout or they would have passed me by.

"Yes?" the lady serving asked. She was portly and rosy cheeked, her hair in deep-set waves and she wore a dark green overall.

"Well?" she shouted again, sharply.

I stuttered.

"Em… a large loaf and an ounce of meat: Spam please."

"I think you mean two ounces, love!" she smiled.

I pressed my lips together and nodded, feeling very embarrassed. As I walked from the shop, I overheard snatches of conversation.

"Yes, they had it really bad."

"How many casualties?"

"They don't know yet."

I noticed only one wooden tray of fresh bread left. I heard a woman's laughter and wondered how anyone could smile at all this havoc.

I stared at parked marmot prams and waved to the babies, playing with their rattles. I dawdled back home walking on fairy feet, then skipping, swinging my string bag. A few more steps and I would be home. I was thinking about my mother and wondering what was the matter with her.

When I gave her the loaf, she snatched it from me and turned away. I think she had been crying. She sank onto the settee.

"Mary," she sniffed and blew her nose, "it's… it's Mrs Dunne, love. She's dead."

Her words seemed to drift away. I answered quickly, "She wasn't in the bread queue. I couldn't help carry her shopping," I whispered. "I'm going to read Brer Rabbit," and I rushed across the room.

When Dad came home, the house smelt of oily paint and turpentine. He pecked Mum's cheek. Mum's reply was, "Jack, don't spill ash everywhere. That room's spotless!"

"And how's my little bird?" He ignored Mum's attitude as he patted my head.

I smiled up at him through watery eyes. He had paint in his hair, on his face and on his arms, but he looked happy. I tried to read my book, but I kept reading the same line over again. "What's this?" Dad was holding up my picture.

"I did it today, Dad," and I proceeded to tell him about it. As I stared at the figures, I caught sight of her hat: I had drawn a bright yellow hat.

"There's Mrs Dunne and I'll never see her again." I broke down and sobbed and Dad held me close to his messy white overalls.

"Don't fret, love. Don't cry." But I needed so much to cry my heart out. Dad caressed my head and I sobbed till my body ached. He sat patiently, whispering to me, "There, there, my little lamb. Look, there're sausages for tea."

Mum was setting out the knives and forks on the table. As I rubbed my eyes, I stared up at her; did she have any feelings?

Yes, I would miss Mrs Dunne very much. When I lay in bed that night and my father was just about to tell me a story, I looked searchingly into his eyes.

"Dad, why did Mrs Dunne die? Why did God take her away?" I felt I wanted to cry again. Dad took a deep sigh as he sat on the edge of my bed. His eyes searched deeply into my patterned wallpaper and, after thinking a moment, he made a bold statement.

"You see, Mary, lots of people die and go to heaven in the war and, sometimes, children like you also die. So, I think God took Mrs Dunne to look after the children." He gave a broken sigh.

"You mean she'll give them a biscuit, too?"

"Yes, love, she'll give them a biscuit, too." Dad bit his lip and looked rather sad and then he gently kissed my forehead. I finally fell asleep, aware of a great contentment from my dad's splendid words.

We had a week of clear days without a raid. A child can quickly forget the nightmare of bombs and sirens, but when I stared at my picture on the wall above the fireplace, where Dad had given it pride of place, I felt a pang of sadness combined with a little joy.

It was now March, a time of spring. The days were fine and dry, but the war seemed to blot out the seasons. Easter would soon be here and the thought of getting an Easter egg made my mouth water. The nights were becoming lighter, but the constant raids on our city made the sky dismal and dull.

March 13th, 1941. It was 3am and we all sat quietly in the shelter, feeling very weary. The guns overhead had been rumbling for over an hour. I couldn't sleep; I stared around me. I could hear the cry of a baby and in the corner was a grey haired old lady, a crocheted shawl resting around her shoulders. She was quietly mumbling, twisting her rosary beads between her limp fingers. The two old men were again playing drafts, forever accusing each other of cheating. My mum was sleeping, and Beryl's mum was caressing her hair, as we all waited for the final siren. We were so desperately tired. There was this silence and we all listened hard. I stared at the space where Mrs Dunne would have sat and I hated the war at that moment. There was a sudden rumble in the distance and then, from out of nowhere, there came this terrific bang. Suddenly, we were all thrown forward from our seats. We were lifted and slowly hurled along the floor of the shelter. There was a sharp pain in my head and then numbness. The women screamed and the old lady fell to her knees and then darkness; the light bulb had shattered. I felt Mum's arms holding on to me.

"It's alright, it's alright." She fumbled in her bag and switched on her torch. I could hear crying, but no-one except Mum spoke. We were all so stunned, wondering what had happened. I licked my lips to feel a fine powdery ash on them. We coughed and spluttered in the darkness, as the debris settled around us. A few torches came on and one of the old men helped the old lady to her feet.

"Did you hurt yourself?" he asked gently.

"Of course not," she exclaimed proudly, "but I've lost my beads."

The old man frowned as he fingered the floor, trying to retrieve his drafts and her rosary. We sat and shivered in the darkness and everything was silent again. We waited and we waited. My forehead felt sore. I must have hit my head in the commotion. Time passed slowly and after the sounds of more distant rumblings had finally died away, the 'all clear' sounded.

We all felt tired and achy as we slowly made our way back to our homes. At least our terrace was still standing! There was the sound of fire engines in the distance and we knew that someone close had become another statistic of this war. The dawn of another day was unfolding and Mum and I fell into our beds, half-dressed, as sleep overtook us.

I awoke with a headache; it was almost midday and I was surprised to see Mum bright and lively.

"Come on, Mary, I think you need a good wash."

All that dust was ground into our skins from last night's ordeal.

"Mam, I wonder what that big blast was?"

"I don't know, love, but it certainly frightened everyone." She eyed me with concern. "'Ere, let's have a look at you." She touched my forehead. "That looks sore!"

I felt a small lump. "It only hurts when I touch it, Mam," I whispered.

Mum rubbed a little butter on the area. "That'll make it better," she beamed.

After a wash and a change of clothes, I felt more wide-awake and I sat in the chair by the fire and wrote about last night's raid in my notebook. I didn't have to go to school while the afternoon.

When Dad walked in, he looked exhausted.

"Oh, Eth, there was a land mine dropped on a shelter in Ellis Terrace. I think most of the people were killed; it was flattened." Then he bit his lip as he stared in my direction. He didn't know I was listening, he looked uncomfortable. "I… I'm sure they will all be saved in time," he added slowly, to reassure me.

I looked into Dad's eyes. "It's alright, Dad. I knew someone got hurt last night, even I bumped my head."

His black features showed a smile at my innocence in all this mayhem. I suppose he knew that I was growing up too quickly, like many other six-year-olds and there was nothing he could do about it. He started to tell us of all the damage in last night's raid, about the bombing at Stoneferry and a landmine in Bricknell Avenue. He sighed deeply. "Oh, what a shambles, Eth." He sank into a chair and threw back his head, his uniform dishevelled.

Seeing Dad so tired, Mum made him a mug of hot tea.

"We heard the big bang, Dad; it shook the shelter," I gasped.

Dad sipped his tea and smiled towards me, as he stood his mug on the floor beside him. I was about to tell him about the way in which we were shaken in the shelter, but within seconds, he was in a deep sleep. He was fully clothed and he never stirred as Mum and I struggled to pull off his heavy boots.

Mum turned the radio down as we listened to a subdued 'Worker's Playtime'. I sat and did some drawing. After about an hour, Dad sighed and grunted; he still looked very tired. He stretched his arms and yawned loudly.

"Can you eat some stew, Jack?" Mum asked gently.

He blinked his eyes, stretching again. "Aye, Eth, that'll be nice." He walked unsteadily into the scullery and rinsed his grimy face; he lifted his limp eyelids and stared around the room.

"Then I'll have to go back. I've volunteered; they need a heavy rescue squad," he sighed. "There was all hell let loose last night, Eth."

I knew what Dad meant. He would probably be looking for bodies and I thought of people still lying motionless under the grey rubble.

It would soon be Easter. At school we were doing lots of projects for the Easter period. Art was my favourite subject, though it was hard to concentrate on skipping bunnies and chicks bursting from eggs, denoting new life, when only the night before, we had sat listening to the bombs intent on destroying life. Proudly, I gave Mum my card and she placed it on the mantelpiece. On Easter Sunday, I came down to breakfast and there was a small brown paper bag on my plate. I opened it eagerly; there was a little note.

It read: 'Dear Mary, we have no egg for you, but happy Easter, love Mum and Dad, kisses'.

I didn't get an egg, but I did get a Mars bar; a whole one to myself: half a week's sweet ration, but Mam wouldn't let me eat it till later that day. Then she gave me a lecture about looking after my teeth, though I quite liked the idea of putting my milk teeth under the doormat, the fairies might bring me more sixpenny pieces.

After Easter Monday, Mum opened her shop again and I was able to help her, only she opened at odd hours because of all the recent raids we had encountered. I loved being in the shop and Mum's business seemed to be thriving. I saw a different side to my mother: she was always in a good mood. We continued to go to the nearest fish shop and buy chips. Again, we would sit behind the velvet curtain and savour their flavour. The customers must have become accustomed to the lasting smell of our vinegary chips and sometimes Mum bought me a ginger parkin for afters. Mum rarely worked a full day in her shop, because we spent so much time in our communal shelter and we were always so tired. Night after night, we settled in the shelter and the month of May was to be the worst bombing on record.

On the 7th and 8th May, 1941, the city of Hull suffered one of the most devastating attacks. Dad would tell us of the deeds of courage he saw and he spoke of his horror, as he had rushed down a street strewn with bodies and then of his relief, to find they were only dummies from a shop window. He seemed to walk about in a constant state of stupor, so tired he was.

The weather was getting warmer and Mum let me wear ankle socks instead of my knee socks, and my ankle strap shoes. Beryl and I were able to play outside more, and with our other friends. We played games of Marbles, Cig Cards, and Jacks. My dad had also brought some very thick rope from the docks, tied it in a loop and suspended from our tall terrace gas lamp and we took turns to swing around at great speed. This was great fun, but it had its drawbacks: sometimes we bumped our heads if we spun around too fast.

I had my sixth birthday: June 24th, 1941. Beryl came for tea. I got new pencils and a drawing book and Beryl gave me a tennis ball. I had a great time as we bounced the ball on the lavatory door. Mum made us a special treat. We sat on the back doorstep and ate homemade chips; she put them in a paper bag like the chip shop chips and they tasted scrumptious. Afterwards, Mum gave us a bag of 'Butterkist' and a glass of cherryade.

After a few days, we had another raid. I had been in bed only a short while, when the air raid siren sounded, but as we were walking to the shelter the all clear siren sounded, so we stumbled back, angry and annoyed at this intrusion into our slumbers. It seemed to be like a mental and physical cruelty, exhausting our wellbeing.

On August 6th, 1941, the King and Queen came to visit Hull. I remember Dad telling me how proud he felt that they were coming to visit our town. It was because of all the devastation to one northern city. They wanted to see how the people of the city were coping and they walked around the debris and the ruins in shock, shaking hands with different dignitaries, talking of people's loss and pain. This visit boosted everyone's resolve and helped them to face whatever was to come. I stood with Mum in the crowd, but I never actually saw them. Dad showed me pictures in the Hull Daily Mail. I read that the day was fine and warm for the royal visit and how the King and Queen had marvelled at the people's bravery in such turmoil. This visit didn't seem to boost my mother's morale, if anything she was becoming distinctly edgy.

The following night, when I sat drawing, she snapped at me, "You do nothing but draw and you don't help me."

Dad opened the back door; he was covered in oily green paint and I ran to him.

"Hello, Dad," I gasped.

"Mary, go to bed," Mum gestured.

Dad smiled. "I'll come up soon, Mary," and he winked at me.
I lay in bed, quietly listening. Mum was shouting at Dad, too.
"Yer tea's all spoilt again, Jack."
"We had to finish this job, Eth," he muttered and then there was silence.

Before I climbed into bed, I switched off my light so I could look out of my window. It was a beautiful, clear night with a huge moon and stars twinkling through the blue velvet sky. The calmness of it all shocked my senses and I found it so hard to believe there was a war going on causing such unhappiness, when I stared at such perfection.

Dad came in and put his arm around me. "What a lovely night, Mary," and we both stared into the heavens.

I thought a moment. "Dad, is the moon far away?"

"Yes, love, and the stars, too. Come on, into bed with you," and his strong arms held me close, as he gently lowered me onto my bed. He now smelt of Brilliantine and soap.

"Will the war end soon, Dad?" I asked earnestly.

"Soon, little bird, soon." As he answered, his face looking doubtful; of course he had no idea. "Can you tell me a story, Dad?"

"Just a tiny one, then," he whispered.

I settled down in-between the blankets and listened to Dad's soothing voice, as he spoke of magic and princesses who were always called Mary!

I had a full night's sleep, but it was just to be a break in the hostilities.

The following evening, we all sat in the shelter once more and listened, as the planes overhead thundered across the sky. Tonight, the bombing sounded quite close. We had been in the shelter for more than an hour and there came this distant whistling.

"That sounds like doodlebugs," Mam whispered, referring to the V-1 flying bombs the Luftwaffe used. After the whistling came a short pause, then great explosions. Our shelter shook and the electric light bulb swayed, as dust filtered into our lungs.

"It's getting closer," the old man shouted. The whistling was overhead. I held on to Mam as the whistling came to a sudden stop…

We waited…

People were counting, "One… two… three..."

Suddenly, a loud thud reverberated through the shelter, as we all bowed our heads and prayed. We coughed and choked, as dust spewed through the air.

"God, that was close," I heard someone whisper.

I felt sure that we were the only people left down our street. The thunder gradually died away as we sat and waited. I suppose we all had snatches of sleep, because we were all mentally and physically exhausted.

There was a look of helplessness around me, as we all rubbed the sleep and the grit from our eyes and the all clear sounded. Everyone sighed with relief and we winced at our cramped bodies as we shuffled, in dignified fashion, through the shelter opening. Grey smog was everywhere, smarting at our eyes.

As my sight adjusted to the eerie light, I could see a deep pink glow towards the end of my street. "There's a fire, Mam!" I shouted.

"Shush," Mum said, "there will be lots of fires, but at least our house is still standing."

As we walked down the terrace, some of the windows were broken and glass crunched under our feet. Our windows had escaped the blast.

As Mum made us a hot drink, she was talking, very fast, about the raid, the bangs and the mess. She went on and on; I think it was her nerves again. As I crawled into bed, I was thinking about Dad.

"I wonder where Dad is, Mam?" I asked earnestly.

"Oh, he'll be alright. Never mind your dad, what about my shop?" she snapped as she pulled the eiderdown up over my shoulders. I turned and I sobbed, heartbroken, into my pillow.

"She doesn't care," I cried, feeling that I hated her at that moment. I must have cried myself to sleep, for when I awoke; Dad was home, safe and sound. I think I was mentally exhausted and I didn't understand the way I was feeling, as my thoughts plunged from one thing to another.

Chapter 11
'Most devastating attacks'

Mum and I set off down the avenue for afternoon lessons; Mum was then going on to open her shop. Newland Avenue was quite busy, the trolley buses were still working and the Co-op milk van buzzed as it passed me by, having delivered all the milk.

There was much activity: wardens wandering around and policemen directing traffic. There was a large crowd of people opposite my school, at the corner of De-Grey Street. Mum was about to take me into school, when I pulled on her arm.

"Mam, can we go and see?"

She shook her head, but her own curiosity got the better of her and we made our way across the road. We stood with all the other people, but I couldn't see anything. I let go of Mum's hand and pushed my way through a crowd of onlookers. I heard them talking.

"It blew my windows out!" one voice said.

"It doesn't bear thinking about," said another.

"Has it gone off?"

What were they talking about? I had to find out. When I reached the front, all I could see was debris. A huge water pipe belched out of the broken pavement, spraying water like a fountain through a haze of smouldering rubble and before me, was a deep crater. It seemed to fall into the centre of the earth! I strained my eyes and there, in front of me, was a black shiny monster with wings. Suddenly, I felt a sharp pain across my cheek; the loud slap rang in my head, along with Mum's screaming, hysterical voice.

"Don't you ever run away again, do you hear?"

I trembled as I started to answer, "I only..."

Mum butted in, "You're a naughty girl." She gripped me tightly around my shoulders and shook me.

"But there's a monster with wings, Mam," I cried, my face burning.

"That's not a monster, that's a 'doodlebug'! And the wings, as you call them, are fins."

She was screeching and her eyes were rabid. Was this deep anger a sign of her love for me? As I sat through my afternoon lessons, my face ached. That night, when Dad kissed me goodnight, he asked me why my face was bruised; I told him I had fallen at school.

On September 7th, 1941, our Prime Minister, Mr Churchill, came to visit Hull; it was another fine day. Dad told me that he had caught a glimpse of him as his car drove past him, towards the Guildhall.

"Dad, why are all these important people coming to Hull?" I asked seriously.

Dad smiled at my interest. "Well, love, Hull and its people have suffered so much bombing lately; I suppose he thinks that it will boost the morale of the people, because he takes such an interest."

I think Dad was right. Dad's heart certainly lifted when he talked about him. I listened to Mr Churchill's speech on the wireless and he stressed that: 'The people must fight the good fight, and we will never give in'.

The wireless was a lifeline for everyone. Various programmes gave people hope in their daily lives and I was no exception. My favourite programme was 'Nature Walks', with Uncle Sam. It was broadcast around 5pm, at teatime. I would listen intently and dream of wonderful countryside as he talked of different birds, animals and insects along his way. I also liked some of the grown-ups' programmes too: Tommy Handley with 'Itma', the Billy Cotton Band Show, 'Wakey, Wakey', or 'The Henry Hall Band': Geraldo and Charlie Kunz played the piano like no other!

There was a lady singer who had the sweetest, clearest voice. Her name was Vera Lynn. She was called the 'Forces' Sweetheart' because she would visit different army camps and sing to the troops. Her singing was broadcast far and wide and she was loved by all. Some of her songs were aptly titled: 'Wishing' and 'We'll Meet

Again'. 'Workers' Playtime' was the greatest favourite. It would be broadcast over Tannoy systems to factory workers on shop floors all over England, during their dinner break. This was a boost to the workers' morale. The wireless maintained a cheerful, encouraging flow of entertainment, bringing joy to millions of demoralised human beings. The Tivoli Theatre was still open and hosted many popular performers: George Formby and Arthur Lucan as 'Old Mother Riley'. They graced the stage in-between the bombing, but not all public houses could stay open, because there was a shortage of beer.

It amazed me how everyone regarded the war as an inconvenience and persevered so much, to go through their daily lives as if everything was normal. I suppose that was what Dad meant when he talked of 'The British Bulldog Spirit'. I saw signs of this every day.

I would walk along Newland Avenue and watch as shopkeepers swept broken glass from the front of their premises. They smiled cheerfully and chalked up signs like: 'Open, Wide Open', laughing in the face of adversity.

It was a fortnight before Christmas. I helped Mum put up a few paper chains in the shop to give it a jolly atmosphere and Mum was quite busy.

After midnight, once more we filed to the shelter. I took my 'Beano' comic and read it for a while, but my eyes felt sore as they strained in the dismal light and I found it hard to concentrate. Again, there were loud, intermittent bangs. We had sat for over an hour, when the warden lifted up the flap and leaned into the opening. In his usual cheerful manner he shouted,

"Everyone okay?"

"Yes," we all shouted in unison.

"Is it bad tonight?" a voice piped up.

"Cottingham Road, I think; quite close!" he answered quickly.

Because we were all talking, we were not prepared for the sudden explosion. The shelter shook and the warden was thrown forward on to his knees.

"Christ!" he cursed in shock, but he picked himself up almost as quickly as he had fallen. "I'll have to go," he shouted breathlessly and he disappeared from the flap.

"Mam, do you think that was our house?"

She didn't answer; she was busy flicking the dust from her lap. I thought how brave the warden was, to go out into the night not knowing where the next target was to be and there were hundreds of brave men like him, including my dad.

"Try to get some sleep," Mum whispered.

We didn't return to our beds till almost 6am, so, because of our lack of sleep, Mum kept me away from school all that day. In a way I was pleased, it meant that I could help her later at the shop.

As we walked along Newland Avenue, Mum spoke to our neighbour, Mrs Allan.

"Who was hit last night?" Mum asked.

"They say Sidmouth Street School was bombed," she answered, wearily.

When we reached Alexandra Road, there were lots of fire engines and ARP wardens around. The pavements were damp and shrapnel was everywhere. Mum pulled on my arm and stopped dead in her tracks; she gasped, her eyes looking skyward.

I followed her eyes. On the lamp posts, coloured paper and rags dangled. We stepped closer: clothing lay in small heaps, steeped in mud and grime.

"Oh, Mary! Oh, no!" Mum was sobbing.

The ground seemed to breathe, as spirals of smoke and dust rose in the air. A land mine had dropped on Mum's shop and parts of the terrace of houses were now piled up where her counter would have been. She pawed the ashes with her foot, gave a little whimper and slid to her knees. She crouched there in the filth and wept quietly. I put my arms around her neck. I didn't know what to do.

"Oh, Mam," I gasped.

We lingered until a warden came to us.

"You'll have to move on, dear," he said gently and he helped Mum to her feet.

"Have you lost someone?"

Mum looked dazed. "It was my shop. My shop!" Her face was red and her eyes puffy, her clothes wet and stained.

He patted her shoulder. "I am so sorry, love. Better go home, have a cup of tea. The men want to knock the remaining buildings down to make it safe, come on," and he coaxed her away.

We walked home in silence; I didn't know what to say to Mum, she was so distraught.

Mum seemed numb, she had gone eerily quiet. She sat in the living room and just stared at the wall. I put the kettle on the gas hob and started to make some tea. This seemed to be everyone's answer to shock: a nice cup of tea. I wanted to hug her and make her feel better, but she defied all affection. All I could think about was how much I would miss sitting at the back of the shop, eating my chips!

When Dad came home, he tried to console her.

She quietly sobbed; all she kept saying was, "You don't understand, nobody understands!" and she cried all the more.

He tried to hug her, but she pulled away. I felt sad too and when I lay in bed that night. I dreamt of the bomb falling from the sky, the sparks, the flames and the clothes floating through the smoky air.

For days, my mum wandered around in a dream and I realised just how much that shop had meant to her. As I wrote about all these events in my little book, I knew that this war would change all of our lives. I wrote of how I hated the Germans, yet there would be a German girl probably thinking the same of me.

Christmas was a non-event; people were too tired to celebrate. Mum hardly spoke, except to chow at Dad for coming in late and having spoilt his tea, but Dad was kind, he talked to her and vowed that he would find her another shop. This seemed to cheer her up a little.

My mother was hard to understand. I didn't know whether I liked her angry or happy, because I felt that she had lost some of her fighting spirit.

We all began to feel a little better because the first three months of 1942 were peaceful, we had no raids and we caught up on lost sleep and reflected upon the year before, when we had been relentlessly bombed. More than anyone, my dad was looking brighter, more alert and I was glad for him. We had three whole months without a raid. It was wonderful to go to school for full days and not fall asleep at my desk. With happy hearts we made Easter cards and hung Easter bunnies around the classroom.

It was the Easter school holidays. Mum, me, Beryl and her mum went out for the day to Pearson Park. There was this wonderful smell of damp grass and a heavy, sweet smell of recently cut privet hedges. It was a joy to be in fresh air and Beryl and I ran onto the grass as if we had been let out of a cage, we felt so happy. Dad had taken two large 2lb jam jars, tied string around the rims, and, with a special knot, he had made handles. He gave us sixpence each to buy fishing nets.

It was the first time I had ever been fishing. Beryl and I leaned along the huge stones around the park pond. We peered into the murky water and beneath, tiddlers and red-breasted sticklebacks darted back and forth, but we couldn't seem to catch anything. I think we were making too much noise, giggling, but we had fun trying.

After a warm, balmy afternoon, we walked home, sporting our jars full of pond water, weed and shiny black water beetles.

Because the raids had subsided for a while, my dad was at home when I went to bed and we had a long cosy chat. I told him about the park and my fishing.

"Dad, I don't understand. Why didn't I catch a fish?"

He smiled at me and his brown eyes twinkled.

"Hmm, well," he whispered, "did you sit very quietly, with your net very still under the water?"

I frowned. "Well, no Dad. We just stirred it with our nets."

"Oh, my little bird, you will never make a great fisherman!" Dad laughed. "Night, night, my love, sleep tight," and quietly, he left the room.

The raids started once more, but the siren only sounded on odd occasions, not every night like last year.

June, 1942, and Monday was to be my birthday. I would be seven years old, but I was still small for my age. Dad turned to me.

"Grab your coat, Mary, we're going out."

"Where, Dad?"

"You'll see! It's a surprise," he grinned, "I don't have to go to work today and we're going for a ride on my bike.

"It's a good job you're still a little sparrow," he laughed, "I know it's your birthday on Monday, but I'll be at work then, so I thought I would take you today."

I was intrigued and looked bemused.

We set off down the avenue. I sat on the saddle on the crossbar and Dad peddled for all he was worth. We had to keep alighting from the cycle to walk along the way, because of certain restrictions where there had been bomb damage. My dad had to be careful so as not to get a puncture in his tyres, but finally we came to the town centre, then we turned down Albion Street.

We were at the museum, a great domineering building of huge proportions with towering pillars at the entrance. Dad rested his bike against the wall and he held my hand as we entered through the large glass doors. I stared, wide-eyed, at walls festooned with gold-framed oil paintings. There was a big, stuffed white bear, baring his teeth with a ferocious expression, so real; I was waiting for him to growl. There were row upon row of glass cases and many other stuffed animals on various stands. Excitedly, I asked Dad lots of questions and he answered every one patiently. The huge room echoed with voices, as we mused at the specimens and history before us. We sauntered through, passing life-like figures. I touched their garments, though I wasn't supposed to. They looked so realistic, I felt that they could almost speak to me.

"Mary," Dad whispered, "we're coming to the last room, I think you'll be surprised, love."

I stared upward and gasped. Before me, hanging spread-eagled from the high ceiling, was a prehistoric monster, a dinosaur. His bones were all pieced together from his head, to his long spine, to his stumpy legs and long tail. His great skeleton stretched from one end of the room to the other.

Dad put his hands on my shoulders. "See, Mary, all his bones are intact."

"What does 'intact' mean, Dad?"

"Well, it means, when he was found, every one of his bones was there, nothing was missing."

I stared at him and wondered what life must have been like when we lived in caves and foraged for food. One tap from that huge tail and our brick shelter would be no more!

When we arrived back home, I couldn't stop talking about the museum. Dad had given me a lovely surprise for my birthday.

My actual birthday was a quiet affair. We had had a raid on Sunday night and it lingered on until the early hours and we all felt a little weary next day, but Mum managed to give Beryl and I a lovely tea. We had potted meat sandwiches, cress and we had some tinned pineapples and custard for sweet. Although the weather was a little showery, Beryl and I had a game of 'Hop Scotch' in the back yard, because Mum had given me some large chalks for my birthday and I wanted to chalk everywhere!

Beryl gave me a most unusual present: a small blue stone, which she had found in amongst the shrapnel. It was very pretty and sparkled when I held it up to the light. Invariably, we ended the evening playing 'Double Ball'. We would chant long verses, as we took our turns to throw the ball. I learnt 'over arms', and 'uppers', and 'dropsy'; all terms we used in our game.

An example of one such verse I learnt was: 'In Leicester Square, 'OVER', there is a school, 'OVER', and in that school, 'OVER', there is a room, 'OVER', and in that room, 'OVER', there is a desk, 'OVER', and at that desk, 'OVER', is where I sit, 'OVER', and learn my A,B,C, 'OVER', 'OVER', 'OVER'……. and so on. Then we would see how long it would take us to do our full ABCs.

The weather improved, and Beryl and I constantly played in our back yard. Beryl would always bring Betsy; her pink dress was looking decidedly shabby. During the school holidays, Mum walked me around the streets, looking out for another shop, but the shops which were empty were bomb damaged.

During the period up to August, we were free from raids. Then we had a short raid in the middle of the night at the very end of August. Dad told us some damage had occurred at the docks, but no one was injured or killed. Then everything went quiet once more and we all enjoyed preparing for the Christmas period.

The grownups tried to celebrate it, if only for the children's sake. My most memorable and favourite present that year was a wooden bat. On it perched six wooden chickens with long wooden necks. Fine string was attached to each neck. All the strings were drawn together down the centre hole on to a lead weight and as I swung the bat gently round, the chicks pecked furiously at the painted grain on the bat's surface.

Our last raid of 1942 was on the 20th December. It only lasted for half an hour. Luckily the siren sounded at 7pm and we were back at home by 8pm, so it was more of a nuisance than anything.

Our next raid was in the middle of January, 1943 and it only lasted an hour and no one was hurt. It seemed to me that the

Germans were flagging, or so I thought, until a few months later, when something happened which was to numb my senses and strike fear into my soul.

Chapter 12
'Dad's cold; a God send'

One night when Dad came home, he was shivering and coughing, he looked poorly. For once, Mum seemed quite concerned for him. He lay on the settee and tried to sleep; he wouldn't eat any tea, he felt too ill.

"I hope we don't have a raid tonight, Eth," he whispered in a hoarse voice.

Mum took a jar of Vick's Vaporub out of the cupboard and loosened Dad's shirt buttons. She gently rubbed Dad's chest with her warm hands.

"Thanks, Eth, that's better."

As Dad rested, in-between bouts of coughing and shivering, he tried to read the evening paper. I sat in the corner of the room watching and I remember thinking, 'Mum does love Dad a little!'

I ran into the hallway, stood on the first tread of the stairs and reached for Dad's overcoat from the hook on the tall hall stand. It was quite heavy, but I managed to lay it over Dad as he rested. Looking up at me, he smiled.

"Why, thanks, Mary. Can you go to bed without a story tonight, love?" then he coughed again and looked very pale.

"Of course I can, Dad," I smiled.

That night, Mum tucked me in, but I had a fitful sleep. I could hear Dad coughing and, come to think of it, I had never seen Dad ill before. I quietly climbed out of bed and knelt down.

"Please, God, make Dad better and thank you for showing Mum how to care for him and making me happy." Did my prayer make sense? I knew it would to God.

I didn't sleep for long before there was the familiar sound of the siren. Dad was at the bedroom door.

"I'm coming with you tonight, Mary."

He held my hand as we all rushed towards the shelter. It was a cool evening; he wore his overcoat and helped me with my gabardine. Our neighbour, Mr Allan, was blowing into his hands.

"It's not cold enough for them up there, is it?" his wife remarked, as she stared above, while she tied her headscarf neatly under her chin. I stared around me. Most people looked angry at yet another disturbance. Dad had another coughing fit. He cleared his throat loudly. I looked at him and beamed.

"This is great, Dad."

He blew his nose, he stared up at me. "What do you mean?"

'Well, I mean, it's nice for you to be with Mam and me, but I wish you didn't have a bad cold!"

"Yes, the wretched cold." He sniffed again.

We all sat waiting and listening.

Mr Allan leaned forward, "There'll be some targets hit tonight! They can't miss, it's so clear."

Dad answered indignantly, "Neither can we."

There was a whistling overhead; I turned to Dad.

"That's a Doodlebug, Dad," I whispered.

Dad just smiled. Of course, he already knew, but I was trying to impress him.

We sat for over an hour and the thunder seemed to subside, but we could hear odd bursts of gunfire in the distance. We all tried to sleep, but poor Dad was constantly coughing, which wasn't surprising, as the air was heavy with cigarette smoke, visible as it danced around the 60watt bulb in the damp ceiling. As we huddled together, our sweat became a vacuum of torrid air. Finally, the 'all clear' sounded and everyone sighed as they stretched.

"Thank goodness, Jack, back to our own beds," Mum remarked.

We were all edging towards the opening: our neighbours, Mr and Mrs Allan, went before us, then Mum, Dad and me. It was wonderful to feel the cold blast of early morning air, even though it was tainted with phosphorous. It was not yet four o'clock, the skies overhead were still dark. We seemed to step into a different dimension. There was this heavy wet fog and all the crisp night air had gone. I held Dad's hand and we slowly stepped out through the shelter opening.

I could barely see Alandale; everything seemed to be in shadow. I could see search lights beaming through the haze and I could hear fire engines trailing their constant whining, but I could hear another sound above it, a deep low pitched humming. Dad and I stared towards the sound above our heads. I could see a tiny light in the distance, peering out of the smoggy air. Coming into view, was a plane.

"It's a plane, Dad!" I shouted excitedly.

Dad suddenly took a deep intake of breath, coughing and spluttering as he shouted, "Quickly, back to the shelter!"

"But, Dad, I…"

Dad ignored my pleas and pulled me towards the shelter opening.

"It's Jerry!" he shouted, using the military term we gave the Germans. His voice was trembling. He dragged at Mam's coat and she almost fell. Mr and Mrs Allan pushed past us into the shelter, and, as we followed, I stumbled and caught sight of the light. It was now bigger and closer and the humming was almost inside my head. Suddenly the ack, ack, ack, of the rear gun juddered, as bullets whizzed through the air only inches past our heads. Mum was screaming as we fell like ninepins and toppled upon one another. Mrs Allan was crying as her hands reached out in the darkness, grasping at the air around her. As I pushed out the palm of my hands, I felt them burn as the grit on the shelter floor grazed the surface of my skin away.

We were all in a state of shock, panting and gasping, sprawled along the shelter floor. We all tried to straighten ourselves up. I got up off my knees and started to brush the dust from my clothes; it was then that I suddenly felt the pain in my hands.

We were all staring at each other in disbelief. Dad was breathless.

"I'm sorry, love, but I had to push you. Are you alright?"

I sobbed a little and as I answered, "Yes, Dad, it was the ground that was hard."

Dad was angry now. "Where the hell did he come from?"

Everyone whispered amongst themselves and waited.

Mrs Allan groaned, "We only just made it, and I think I've bruised my hip."

Mum suddenly spun round and almost spat at Mrs Allan, only I couldn't see her anger in the darkness.

"I hope you have," Mum began, "What about us? Pushing past us like that! We could have been killed!" Her voice was high pitched. "Poor Mary's hurt her hands."

I could hear Dad telling Mum to calm down, he didn't want a row with the neighbours.

"Were they real bullets?" shouted the old woman with her rosary beads.

"What do yer think they were?" the old man answered, angrily.

"Were they really shooting at us, Dad?"

He looked towards me, "Yes, Mary, I'm afraid they were." He gave a deep sigh. "We'll wait a bit before we go back outside."

We waited patiently and after a few minutes, Dad spoke again, "I'm going to look out now, to see if it is safe for us to go home."

He ventured towards the opening and peeped out, gingerly. He caught his breath, as he saw some people lying very still. He swallowed hard and listened; he couldn't hear any aircraft overhead. He turned to us in the shelter. "Just wait a minute, I won't be long".

He ran to the first body, that of a young woman. He couldn't see where she was injured, so he put his index finger on her neck and felt for a pulse. Suddenly, she jumped and turned her blackened face towards him.

"Have they gone?" she gasped.

"Yes, are you hurt?" Dad replied.

She sighed and stretched. "I... I don't think so. I just fell to the ground and look, look, my gas mask!" She held out her gas mask case. Almost through its centre were two bullet holes.

"Good God, that could have been me!" And under all her grime, she went pale.

As Dad helped her to her feet, others stirred. People whispering, disbelieving what had just happened. They didn't seem to be hurt, just shocked. Dad was thankful for that and he turned to go back to the shelter, but a few feet to one side, lay the body of an old man. He lay partly off the ground, slumped over a birdcage. He was very still. Dad lifted his limp body and laid him gently along the ground. He could see the scarlet stains on his waistcoat and his legs. He had been peppered with bullets.

"No!" he whispered, letting out a deep, quivering sigh. He slowly pressed his fingers on the old man's eyelids to cover his staring eyes, then Dad took off his overcoat and laid it over him. He stood up and watched his own breath as it feathered the air before him; he felt so helpless, so inadequate, as tears welled in his eyes. The dead man looked about the same age as his father. The hot tears fell down Dad's cheeks and he lifted his fist to the grey skies and in an angry, broken voice he shouted: "This Bloody War!"

Chapter 13
'Mouse, Mumps and the Morrison'

Mum and I stood at the shelter opening.

"Jack, where's your coat?" she snapped.

Dad's voice was breaking; he rubbed hard at his cheeks, "Oh never mind about that, Eth. Come on. We can go home now, it's safe."

We filed out, quietly whispering, gasping and staring at the shapeless form beside us. The old lady made a sign of the cross as she passed by.

"Oh, dear, dear, dear," she cried in despair.

Dad held the birdcage and we walked home slowly.

As Mum bathed and bandaged my hands, she talked to Dad.

"We're not even safe after the 'all clear', Jack."

"I know, Eth. I'm surprised more people weren't hurt."

My hands felt a little better now. Mum had rubbed them with Vaseline and the soreness was going away.

"Dad, I felt the bullets whizzing past my ears; wait till I tell them at school." I was feeling excited, I didn't grasp the implications.

Dad rinsed his tears away under the cold water tap, held his head in the towel for a second and quivered as he sighed. I thought of the past moments, then I realised: if we hadn't run away and Dad hadn't pulled us towards the shelter, we could have been killed.

"You saved our lives, Dad!" I whispered, wide-eyed. I felt so proud of him at that moment. But Dad bowed his head in sadness and replied softly, almost in a whisper, "Yes, but not everyone's life. Not quite, Mary." He sighed.

I opened the cage door and lifted out the pale blue budgie, his body was cold and limp.

"Dad, there isn't a bullet wound."

Dad turned to look at the small bird. He stroked his head. "Maybe he died of shock, poor thing."

I held him high in my cupped, bandaged hands. "Look, Mam?"

Mum wouldn't come closer, said she was afraid of feathers, so she stayed at the other side of the room. It was so pretty.

Dad took an old teacloth out of the sideboard drawer and gave it to me. "Wrap him up and we will bury him tomorrow. Now, to bed with you!" He blew me a kiss. "And I hope you don't catch my cold, though it doesn't seem so bad now."

He rubbed his chin. "You know, Eth, if I hadn't had a cold, I wouldn't have been with you tonight." He shivered as he thought of the consequences. "I'll never grumble again!" He lifted his head, looking beyond the ceiling, "I think someone is watching over us." And he pecked Mum's cheek with great affection.

I didn't know the old man who had died, but Mum said that he lived alone in one of the terraced houses across the road from our house. It seemed so unfair and uncanny to be shot down in our street with real bullets and it was ironic to think that if he had stayed inside his house, he would still be alive now and his little budgie would be singing.

We only had a small front garden; I used our old coal shovel and dug a small hole. I laid a piece of newspaper in the bottom of the hole, then I gently laid the swaddled budgie along its surface. I pushed the soil over him, gently. Firmly, I patted it down with my fists because the palms of my hands were sore. At the foot of the small mound of earth, I planted a twig, shaped like a cross. This gave me pause for thought; I didn't even know the bird's name! That night I drew a picture of a blue budgie and at the bottom of the page I wrote: 'Here lies a little bird who has gone with his master to heaven.'

Even Mum said it was a nice thought.

I went to school in the afternoon, still feeling tired and in shock, but I felt quite fussy to have two bandaged hands. I enjoyed the rapture and interest of my classmates as to how I had hurt them.

My dad's ears must have burned as I proudly recalled his actions that night. Friends gathered around me, hanging onto my every word, but, I'm afraid I did exaggerate somewhat. I had a tale to tell and for a time, I felt that I was the centre of attention and why not? It was about my dad and I loved him.

I still managed to draw, even though my hands were sore. I did pictures with planes and bullets whizzing through the air and figures running away with fear on their faces.

I had many restless nights, bad dreams, but Dad would always come and comfort me. He would sit on the edge of my bed and talk for a long time. He never dismissed any of my constant questions. It seemed that since I had seen the poor old man, to me as a child, I was beginning to understand the true meaning of all this bloodshed. But, what I couldn't understand was, why did a poor old man have to die? I felt that there was no reasoning to it all. I was growing up fast and I tried hard to reason the logic of this hatred between the enemy and ourselves.

Soon it was to be my birthday again. As I thought about it, I could think of no greater present than last year, when Dad had taken me to the wonderful museum. As usual, Mum and Dad gave me a lovely surprise: my first real handbag. It was white plastic with a zip and a sling shoulder strap, and inside was a matching white purse that housed a shiny sixpence. I filled the bag with my things: the pretty stone that Beryl had given me last year, a coloured hanky, a small notebook, a pencil, my marbles and cig cards. My grandma Emmett had sent me a cardboard doll and paper clothes for me to cut out. Beryl and I enjoyed playing with that. Mum gave Beryl and I a lovely tea, and Grandma Thompson had sent shortcake biscuits as a treat. We ended the day playing 'Double Ball' on the lav' door, before Beryl went home.

I had had a great birthday.

I felt warm and contented when I went to bed that night, but it didn't last for long.

The siren sounded just after midnight and we seemed to spend half of the night in the shelter, as the bombs whizzed overhead. Finally, I clambered into bed around 5 am.

At least I was able to go to school in the afternoon and Mum let me take my new bag to show to my friends.

Mum and I were sat having tea when Dad walked in; I hadn't seen him since yesterday. His cold was better now, but he looked extremely tired and he looked rather subdued and sad. Mum pushed a plate of sausage and mash in front of him and I wondered what was going on in his head as he sighed to himself.

I awoke, suddenly, to a loud scream and it was morning. The night had passed without a raid, but as I crept down the stairs I felt a little apprehensive: why had Mum screamed?

I walked into the living room to see Mum sitting on a dining chair, her knees tucked under her chin, her feet resting on the spindle beneath. She didn't look up, but peered along the floor.

"Th... there's a mouse, Mary! There's a MOUSE!" she blurted out.

"Is there, Mam? Where?" I immediately dropped to my knees and peered along the floor, feeling excited. Mum was quite hysterical.

"The horrible thing ran across the floor near to your toy box."

I stared at Mum in amazement. I thought she was afraid of nothing, but she was clearly in a panic.

"I think the mouse will have run away, Mam. It will be frightened of us."

Mum was indignant, "This is a clean house, why have we got a mouse?" As she protested, she gingerly pushed a sweeping brush along the coconut mat and after a few minutes, she calmed down.

"Your dad will have to set a trap, Mary," she screeched, as she passed me some toast. "Come on, you'll be late for school"

"Mam, if Dad could catch it, could I have it for a pet?"

Mum lifted her head slowly, looked up to the ceiling for guidance and she blew through her lips. "Mary," she sighed in disgust.

I smiled as I ate my crusts, then I suddenly realised why we had a mouse. That night, I took out all of my toys from my toy box. I struggled and tipped the box on its side; there were no crumbs, but there were lots of black bits, maybe mouse droppings? I quickly swept them onto a shovel and discarded them. I don't think we ever saw the mouse again.

We had a few days' respite, then more raids began. Everyone seemed weary and unsure; each time we left the shelter after the 'all clear', we felt afraid to venture back home.

At meal times, when Dad was at home, he seemed to be growing extremely anxious. I heard brief snatches of conversation.

"We'll buy one, Eth."

"We'll have to get our name on the list, Jack."

"But we can't afford one."

"We will have to, the sooner the better," Dad answered finally.

Each night this seemed to be the thrust of the conversation, then Dad would set off on his bike into the night.

The raids continued and about three of my five days at school were only half days. There was a great shortage of paper and our exercise books were filled to capacity, as we wrote in-between our first lot of writing. Sometimes I couldn't understand what I had first written, the writing was so compact!

It was almost Christmas again and before our school holidays, our teacher showed us how to make trimmings and paper lanterns, which we painted. We left them on our desks for the glue to dry out and the next day, we were to take them home for the Christmas holiday, but we had a bad raid in the Newland Avenue area.

I felt saddened when I looked on my desk; my golden lantern was now a sooty mess, so we had no trimmings that year. The raids were so frequent that Christmas was but a short break in the hostilities once more.

The new year of 1943 began quietly. Everyone seemed totally exhausted and worn out, but we tried to carry on in true British fashion. Dad came home from the docks early one night, his face beaming.

"Look what I've got, Eth." He held out a parcel in newspaper.

Mum laid it on the table and, as she opened it, small cubes of ice dropped from the wrapping. Inside was a huge haddock, its eyes staring into space. Mum stepped back, but her mouth watered. We hadn't eaten fish for a long time, though fish wasn't rationed, it was very scarce. Like many of the little treats Dad brought home, she never questioned him about it. Mum gave Beryl a portion to take home to her mum and for the next few days, we ate like kings.

It was the middle of January when the raids started once more and the weather was biting cold, winds and driving rain. The snow was yet to come. It was just before midnight when we made our first trek to the shelter. Water ran down the walls and the seats were very damp. Mum sighed discontentedly, as we shuffled along the bench seat. At least the shelter was warm with our bodies, as we huddled together.

The thunder started straight away and we sat quietly and waited. The shelter was packed to capacity, we couldn't even stretch our legs. An old man puffed on his pipe and clouds of smoke billowed into our nostrils, as his tobacco glowed red in the stagnant air. Around the 60 watt bulb hung the blue haze.

The waiting dragged on and on.

People yawned and coughed and babies whimpered as they tried to sleep, but above it all, a camaraderie could be felt that transcended the problems of each individual as displayed by the sociability of everyone and the patience in their voices. There seemed to be this togetherness of minds; we all knew each other's hopes and fears.

Almost two hours passed until the 'all clear' sounded and most of us groaned as we stretched to walk back home.

After that night, Jerry went quiet and Easter was enjoyed without a raid. The weather changed and became warmer. We all felt so much better after uninterrupted sleep and Dad began to work fewer hours.

It was Monday morning and I should have been in school, but I had felt poorly all that weekend: my neck hurt and my glands were swollen. Mum said she thought I had the mumps, so she kept me off school. She didn't take me to the doctors, said she couldn't afford the fee and she knew how to treat mumps anyway. I just had to be kept at home and have plenty of warm drinks and rest. I was unable to play with Beryl for a few days because I was infectious, but I still felt well enough to sit and draw.

I was struggling with a large jigsaw; the room was cosy and warm. In the background, the wireless was starting the programme, 'Worker's Playtime'. The only other sound was the cracking from the fire as Mum poked at the embers and tiny sparks shot up to the back of the chimney, adjoining the hanging soot. Suddenly, there was a loud rap at the front door. I jumped and looked up. "Mam?"

"I know, I heard," she snapped.

As she went to answer the door, I stood and watched from the doorway. She opened the front door to a tall, weather-beaten, moustached man. He had a big grin on his face.

"The 'Morrison', love, where would you like it?" The man who was garbed in navy overalls, pushed past a bewildered Mum, then he stopped in his tracks and turned, "You are Mrs Thompson, aren't you?"

Mum was still in shock.

"Good heavens, that was quick! My husband said we would be waiting for ages!"

He beamed and pointed with his clipboard, "Which room, love?"

Mum's cheeks flushed as she answered, "Er… the front parlour, please."

Another man followed him inside. He was of slighter build, but he must have been strong, as his arms were laden with iron blocks.

"Mornin'," he whispered.

What was it, this Morrison? I had to know.

"Come on, Arthur, let's roll back this 'ere carpet," the bigger man shouted.

"I'll take everything out of your way," Mum blundered. She quickly retrieved photo frames, a vase of plastic flowers and an ashtray from above the piano, "I'll leave you to it then and I'll make you some tea."

"Smashing," was the reply.

I dawdled towards the table and attempted my jigsaw once more, but I was burning with curiosity. I could hear lots of noise as metal resounded with metal. I stepped back into the hallway; I just had to know what was happening.

The hallway was now full of different strips of iron. I stood beside the door, my head on one side and my tongue tasting my bottom lip, my hands twisting at the hem of my skirt. One man was whistling, but no apparent tune. He looked towards me and clicked his lips. I looked down at my toes, feeling embarrassed.

The men were putting pieces together, rather like a giant 'Meccano' set. One man held the parts together, whilst the other man pushed big screws into marked holes and turned an incredibly large spanner over the nuts and bolts.

It was beginning to take shape. It was about the size of a double bed and about three feet deep and all around it was a thick mesh wire; it was like a giant cage. My mum walked in with two mugs of hot tea, which she placed on the mantelpiece. The moustached man leaned against the wall.

"Another one finished, Arthur." He gazed at me, "Do you want to climb in it, duck?"

He sipped noisily at his tea, then he popped a cigarette into his mouth and lit it, drawing hard, then sighing smoke as he breathed out.

"Is it a shelter?" I asked shyly.

He smiled, "Yer, you get a big mattress in the bottom and it'll be all cosy, like."

Mum chuckled, "It didn't take you very long!"

"Oh, we build about three a day, love," he sighed. "If you'll just sign here?" and he held out his clipboard to Mum. She signed it readily.

As the two men walked through the front door, the smaller one turned his head and gestured,

"You'll feel nice and safe in there and no mistake."

Mum felt very grateful and watched them walk away. "Thanks," she shouted.

After they had left, we both stared at the incredible cage, which half-filled our front room, but with all the strong mesh around it, I didn't know how to crawl into it.

"We'll have to wait for your dad to come home, Mary."

I pulled a face and sighed, "I suppose so."

Dad came home around 6 pm.

"Gosh, it's freezing out there tonight, Eth."

"Dad," I yelled, I was so excited, "we've got a big cage in the front room and it's a shelter of our own."

"Hi, little bird. Have you been good and are you feeling better?"

"Yes, Dad and I've finished my jigsaw, look."

He had partly undone his once-white overalls and his shoulder straps dangled along the stone of the scullery floor as he made his way to the table.

"That's good, Mary," he replied, as he admired my picture of kittens in a basket.

Mum sighed loudly, "Jack, do take off those filthy, oily overalls."

He looked at me as he answered, "Alright," then he winked and his tired eyes sparkled, "then we'll have a look at this 'ere shelter."

He seemed to let Mum's constant nattering pass over his head. As he stood in the front room doorway, he rubbed his head and stared at the green iron and steel monstrosity.

"It's bigger than I thought it would be, Eth. And you're right, Mary, it does look like a cage, doesn't it?" Then he put his arm around my shoulder. "But I don't care what it looks like as long as it keeps you both safe."

"Can we get in it, Dad?" I asked, impatiently.

"After… after tea," he whispered, then he yawned and sank back in a chair.

It was then I realised how tired he must have felt. I broke up my jigsaw and put the pieces back in the box. Mum made me wash my hands, (they were so dirty from touching all the metal on the shelter), then I helped set the table for tea, but my head was aching.

Later, Dad managed to drag the double bed mattress downstairs and, with a struggle, he pushed it into the 'Morrison'. Mum laid a large blanket on top of the mattress, then a flannelette sheet and she tucked it in all around the sides. Dad then had a short nap on the settee before he had to go back on duty.

While he rested, Mum and I made a list of what was to be left in the shelter: Mum's insurance policies, rent book, her handbag and a torch, a holdall bag containing a change of clothing, towels and toiletries and of course our chamber pot and toilet paper. I had my own oddments: my diary, drawing book, pencils, my new hand bag, my toy panda and my favourite story book, Brer Rabbit, not forgetting a small torch of my own.

Mum also packed a few snacks of cream crackers, cheese, a packet of 'Rich Tea' biscuits and a large lemonade bottle of fresh water. She said that this would sustain us if a bomb dropped on our house and we were trapped under rubble for a short while. I pushed that thought out of my mind, I could only think of how cosy and snug it all seemed. It was rather like we were hiding in a big den. As I sat, cross-legged, in the centre of the mattress, Mum bent down and looked me in the eye.

"Tonight, Mary, we can come to bed and if the siren bellows, we can stay put!"

As soon as Mum had stocked the shelter and prodded the pillows, I couldn't wait for bedtime. Dad kissed me good night before he went out, then I squatted in the corner of the Morrison with my torch in one hand and my pencil in the other, but I didn't draw for long, I had too much of a headache. Finally, I curled up and fell asleep, aware of a new-found contentment. Later, I knew Mum had lain beside me as I heard a muffled sound of the wire mesh being pushed into place.

I felt so refreshed and much better the next morning; there had been no raid. I wanted to stay in the shelter, but Mum tossed me out, while she straightened all the bedding. She seemed in high spirits as she worked about the house.

I missed playing 'Cat's Cradle' with my friend Beryl, but Mum said that if I saw her I might give her the mumps, so I sat and played alone. I started to feel a little better and did some drawing. This time I drew the 'Morrison', with Mum, Dad and I peeping from inside.

Mum gave me lots of soup, for it was easier to swallow. We all slept soundly and it was very snug in our caged bed. I kept having snatches of sleep during the following days and my mumps finally went away. At last, Mum let me go out to play.

As I walked down our back passage, I saw my friend, Beryl. We stood and talked as our breath pounded the sharp morning air.

"Do you still live with your auntie?" I asked.

She eyed me and sighed, "I suppose we'll live there forever now, but my mam has talked about going to Withernsea, to my other auntie's house. But we didn't have a raid last night, did we?"

I smiled excitedly, "Hey, come to my house, I've got a den!"

Beryl looked intrigued.

Back at home, Mum was standing by the sink, her arms steeped in soapsuds.

"What the…?" she gulped, as we ran past her.

We both stood panting, peering into my front room.

"Look!" I gasped.

Beryl's eyes widened.

"It's like a giant cage at the zoo. It's great fun, Beryl, we don't have to go to the shelter and we have lots to eat and we have a picnic while the bombs drop!" Then I took a breath! But when I looked at Beryl, she was quiet and frowning; she was thinking about her house.

"But, if a bomb dropped on your house, what would happen?"

I put my head on one side and thought pensively.

"Well, this would still be standing and…" I paused for effect, "we would be intact. Isn't it smashing?" I grinned.

We were just about to crawl in, when Mum shouted from the doorway.

"You dare to take one more step inside that 'Morrison' and I'll skin you alive! Come on the both of you, find something else to do."

We both smiled at each other and walked slowly into the living room. Beryl pulled out her loop of string from her pocket and we sat by the inviting fire and played 'Cat's Cradle'.

Chapter 14
'The Cruel Raids'

The raids on our town were less frequent and the classrooms were full. There was an air of contentment around the school. I suppose everyone felt happier because they were less stressed and tired. The March winds came along and the weather was improving all the time. Although my dad still went out each night after work, he still found time to tell me stories, and now I could also read to him from my storybooks. He would give me two pence a week to buy the edition of 'Sunny Stories' by Enid Blyton.

As I lay in bed at night, the ticking of the alarm clock seemed very loud in such a confined space, but like everything, I grew used to it. I loved this big den, but I missed seeing Beryl and all the different people from the shelter; I missed listening to the many and varied conversations. We had only had one raid since we began sleeping in our new shelter, it was almost as if Mr Hitler had known we had purchased a shelter and he had decided it would have been a waste of time to bomb Alandale.

We were now into June, and Dad suggested a treat before my birthday; it was a Saturday.

"I know it isn't your birthday for two weeks, but I have some free time. Would you like to go to the Museum, again, Mary?"

"Oh, Dad, it would be great," I replied quickly.

"Well then, off we go, though we will have to go on the 62 trolley, because you are growing too big for that bike, Mary," he laughed.

There it was: the huge columns, the great bear beaming, the exhibits, fossils, and Roman relics, all the glass cases. And I lingered for an age staring at my dinosaur; it was as exciting as my last visit, only this time I was a little older and a little wiser. I would write reams about my wonderful day.

That night, I sat by the table and did some sketching. I drew a picture of the majestic building with its towering columns, with a man and a girl entering the huge doorway.

As my birthday drew nearer, I found myself reflecting. The last five months had been so reassuring to me that I felt that this war was coming to an end, but I was wrong. I listened to Dad as he talked to Mum after reading the Hull Daily Mail. He read that the Germans had acquired a new type of bomb and that made him feel uneasy.

People were now rested, but there was a foreboding in the air. Everyone prayed that this lull in the bombing could mean the coming of peace.

It was 23rd June, 1943 and tomorrow would be my birthday, I would be 8 years old. I crawled into the shelter early that night and Mum let me read by my torchlight. I felt excited as I thought about my birthday, for Mum had promised me a real cake and Beryl was coming for tea. I soon fell into a sound sleep.

Suddenly, I was awoken by the sound of rain on the front room window. I lay for a long time, listening. But the mesmerising sound of the rain on the window pane was broken as the air raid siren began to wail. I felt Mum jump and she clicked on her torch shining it in my face.

"Oh, you're awake," she whispered.

"I've been awake ages, Mam. Is this really a raid?"

"Yes," she whispered.

We lay still and waited. We could hear a crackle of artillery in the distance, then two loud bursts, one after the other and thunder rumbled.

"Oh, Mary, I thought the raids had stopped in January."

"I did, too, Mam. And it's my birthday tomorrow." As if that would make any difference to Mr Hitler!

I could hear the peeling of the bells from a fire engine or an ambulance and the rain still washed our windowpanes. We both listened for a few more minutes, then Mum switched off her torch and we gradually dozed off.

Morning brought a blinding brightness after all the rain. Mum stirred and got up quietly and I fell asleep once more, as she dressed and made breakfast.

I awoke to voices. I walked into the living room; Dad was sitting in the easy chair, his hands around a steaming mug of hot tea. He was covered in soot, his face streaky, his eyes like black marbles and the whites of his eyes were red and sore from smoke fumes. He stared deeply into the coconut matting, shaking his head. He continued shaking his head as he looked towards me in the doorway. He looked so tired, so forlorn; there was no cheerful smile from him. I put my fingers to my lips; I knew there was something wrong. I didn't speak, I just waited.

Mum sat beside him, her elbows resting on the tablecloth, her chin leaning on her fists. She was quiet and staring into space.

"Dad?" I questioned.

Dad blinked, as if he had been awoken from a dream. He gave a heavy sigh.

"Oh, the city centre was an inferno last night, Eth, an inferno."

"There was a red glow from all the fires. Oh, God, it was awful! Incendiaries everywhere; as fast as one fire was put out, another started. We couldn't cope, we couldn't do anything, it... it was useless!"

Dad felt inadequate, he was blaming himself for this war! He rested his mug on the table and held his head in his hands. I knelt beside him and pulled on his arm.

"Dad," I whispered gently. I didn't know what to say. As he moved his hands, his face glistened with tears.

"Mary."

I put my arms around his neck and we held each other in a fond embrace. Mum was very quiet, as she filled the sink with hot water and she gently coaxed Dad into undressing. Finally, he tried to wash all his anguish away. He managed to eat some toast, then he climbed into the 'Morrison' and fell into a deep slumber.

I think my dad was suffering from nervous exhaustion. Just when he seemed to be less tired, it was all starting again.

I could see that he was too upset to wish me a happy birthday. I felt very concerned to see my dad so unhappy. I noticed that Mum was anxious too, but I felt better when I looked at all my nice cards.

Mum looked towards me. "Mary, don't worry about your dad, he'll be all right. Here's your present: Happy Birthday." She gave me a paper carrier, inside was a drawing book and pencils and a top and whip.

I had a lovely day. I didn't have to go to school while the afternoon and Beryl came for tea. The day was fine and warm, so Mum let us have our tea outside and while we played with my top and whip, she cooked us homemade chips. She put the chips in paper bags, with lots of salt and vinegar. We sat on our back doorstep. The chips tasted scrumptious. We drank hot cocoa and Grandma Thompson had sent shortcakes and tarts.

Lastly, Mum brought out a small chocolate cake, but we both felt too full, so Mum sliced a piece and wrapped it for Beryl to take home. We talked, played 'Cat's Cradle' and giggled till dusk.

Dad was in the scullery, he looked rested. He was sitting on the bath lid, cleaning his boots.

"Mary, I was too tired to think this morning, but I'm better now. Did you have a nice birthday, love?"

"Oh, yes, Dad," I replied quickly.

Dad brushed vigorously over the toe of his boot as he spoke, "I hope I didn't upset you when I came home, it's just that sometimes I get a little overtired, you know?" I knew what Dad meant and I knew that what he had just said was an understatement. He pushed his boots to one side and looked serious. "Mary, I have some bad news, love. It's er… the museum; I'm afraid it's gone, it was bombed last night. One or two columns are still standing, but it took a direct hit, incendiaries, everything. It's in ruins, love. Everything; gone in seconds." He bowed his head.

I felt stunned. "Oh, Dad," I cried.

Dad put his hand on my shoulder. "I'm so glad we went to see it, Mary."

I thought about the dinosaur, the big bear, all the relics and the wonderful glass cases.

"But, Dad, maybe...," I burst into tears.

"It was burnt to the ground, love, we couldn't save it. I'm sorry, Mary."

Now I knew why Dad was so unhappy when he arrived home.

"Lots of large buildings were gutted last night, love and the museum was one of them. Oh, the havoc, the waste." Then he sighed once more. "Today we are going to see if there is anything to salvage. I'll have to go, Mary," he whispered. He tucked his little finger under my chin, lifting my head and kissed my forehead. He shouted goodbye to Mum and closed the back door behind him.

When I climbed into bed that night, I asked Mum why she hadn't told me about the museum. She said that she didn't want to spoil my birthday; I suppose she had a point.

I tossed and turned with jumbled feelings. I had had a lovely birthday, but the day had ended with sadness. The museum was now just a memory and I felt a hatred for the pilots who had dropped the bombs on my museum. My diary was filled with pouring resentment and anger.

The sun still shone, the weather was glorious and the raids stopped once more. A fortnight passed by and every night, Beryl and I played double ball against the lav' door. It would soon be the summer holidays.

Dad was looking less tired and everyone enjoyed the sunshine. People worked on their allotments and vegetable plots and many families were almost self-sufficient, growing their own vegetables, potatoes, onions, cabbage, and sprouts; all to help the war effort.

Mum was over the shock of losing her second-hand clothing business and I was trying to get over losing my museum.

One day, I went with Mum to see another shop in Waterloo Street, off Fountain Road, but it looked like a shell of a building rather than a real shop, so Mum didn't make any plans.

"I don't think I'll ever find a shop like Alexander Road, Mary," she sighed.

I missed it too.

As we were close to Fountain Road, we called in to see Grandma Thompson, to say hello. The usual smell greeted us in the doorway: fresh baking. She welcomed us with her cheery smile and we sat drinking hot tea and devouring buttered scones. This made me think about Aunt B, but that was such a lifetime ago.

Granddad came in from the hospital and he was quite surprised to see us. As usual, he greeted my grandma with an affectionate peck on her cheek. Mum told him about the shop and as they chatted, Granddad proceeded to light and draw from his pipe. He pushed my drawing book towards me. I was about to start to draw when Mum butted in.

"Mary, we ought to be going now." She looked into my pleading eyes, "Well, just a little longer, or your Dad will wonder where we are."

I didn't answer, but I grinned as I thought Mum was thinking about the furore caused when we stayed with my other grandma in Skidby.

The front door opened and suddenly, my two aunts, Aunt Lilly and Aunt Cathy, burst in. They both looked like Grandma, only they were thinner. Auntie Lilly smiled at me out of the corner of her eye, just the way my Dad used to do, her mannerisms were the same.

"My, but you're good at drawing, just like your Dad," she mused, as she leant over my shoulder. "We've just brought you some mouse traps, Mum," Auntie Cathy shouted.

"We can't stay, left the kids playing in the yard."

I blinked. "Have you got a mouse, Grandma?" I asked quickly.

Grandma was rubbing her hands on her apron. "Why, bless yer, lass, I think I've got more than one. When I open my oven door, first thing, a mouse leaps out." But she just laughed, unconcerned.

My mum visibly shuddered as she stared at the scones on the table. I just grinned to myself. My aunts only lived a few terraces away. I had three cousins, Victor, Tony and Marlene, who were evacuated, but Victor and Tony were now back at home.

The house was noisy; Granddad was browsing over his betting in the Sports Mail, as we all talked with one another and Grandma made more cups of tea. The back door was wide open and the house was full of life. The siren took us all by surprise; it seemed to echo through the house.

Granddad looked up, "Good, lord, he's early isn't he?"

The aunts caught their breath. They seemed to shout together, "We'll have to go, Mum, see you in the shelter," and they dashed out of the door.

Mum's eyes grew wide, as she pulled me from my chair. "What shall we do?"

Granddad calmly assured her, "You can come with us to our shelter. I'm sure it won't last long; it's probably a false alarm anyway."

Grandma pulled on her big brown cardigan and snatched her bag off the dresser. Granddad still held onto his paper and he held my hand as we walked towards the communal shelter. It was the same as ours down Goddard Avenue: dark and dingy and the odour was the same, too.

My aunties were already there and my cousin Victor, who was nearly five years old, was sitting next to his brother, Tony, aged three years.

"This is our shelter," Victor grunted, disapprovingly. Auntie Lilly nudged him and shot him an angry look.

I couldn't believe we were having a raid, it was a fine night and only around 6 pm. The shelter was quite full, so I sat on Mum's knee. It seemed to be full of women and children, many of the Dads were on duty, serving in the forces like my Uncle Victor, in the Navy and my Uncle Billy, in the army. Overhead, the bombers could be heard. So it wasn't a false alarm after all!

We sat crouched, listening and the noise was growing louder, sounding close by. Granddad turned to Grandma.

"It's close, Jane."

She looked his way and nodded her head. Then she reached out for my hand. Our bodies started to jump as the thunder was getting nearer, until it sounded almost overhead. A whoosh sound filled our ears and a loud thud crackled through our heads. We all screamed as the shelter seemed to sway, like some giant hand had lifted us off the ground and then put us down again. This all happened within a few seconds.

The tiny stained light bulb dimmed, then went out altogether. Grit stung at our faces and the air was black. We coughed, gasped and spluttered. Tony and other children were crying. As I rubbed my eyes, I could only make out shadows. I was still on Mum's knee and she found her voice.

"I haven't got my torch."

Granddad spoke authoritatively, "We must all be calm. Stay where you are. We must wait. It was close, but we're all alright."

Everyone felt more relaxed after his words and we waited. There was some coughing and babies whimpered and people's breathing was laboured, as we were all aware of the closeness of that last bomb. As I sat there in the semi darkness, I heard Grandma whisper to Granddad.

"Do you think it was our…."

Granddad shushed her, "Don't, Jane, it will be alright." Of course he didn't know, but didn't want to upset her.

The thunder seemed to drift away and we sat for ages, feeling cross and apprehensive.

"I wonder where that bomb dropped, Mam," I whispered.

"We'll soon know, Mary."

There was a sudden rustle and the sacking over the doorway lifted and a shaft of light pierced the sooty air, revealing our dusty clothes and grimy features.

"Everyone okay?" The ARP warden flicked his torch in our direction.

Granddad answered, "We're alright, is it bad?"

"Afraid so, terrace up there. Hope the families were in the shelter; flattened, it is!"

I looked at Grandma and Granddad; they hugged one another. Granddad leaned towards the opening, whispering.

"Is it Bohemia Terrace?"

The warden thought a minute, "Oh, no, that one's okay. I think the raid's nearly over, but wait for the all clear. It's crazy out 'ere! I've got to go," and he disappeared.

We were returned to the dimness, as the sacking dropped over the opening. The thunder had now abated and there were different noises: revving, wailing of sirens, but we dared not go out until the all clear sounded. Quite some minutes passed before we were able to leave the shelter. I was about to stretch to get up, when Granddad slipped his hand in mine.

"Wait, wait a minute, Mary." I think he was bracing himself for the shock to come. Everyone was talking quietly, feeling very shaky and tired and we slowly edged our way towards the slant of light. We all piled outside the shelter, wrenching our necks to see ahead. Our end of the street was untouched except for grit and shrapnel strewn around, but a few yards further down was a haze of smoke, fumes and flames. Fire engines, their motors labouring, belched out water to quench the flames. The putrid smell of phosphorous and ash stung the back of my throat. I coughed to clear the taste from my mouth. Wardens and policemen were dashing back and forth, all in disarray. Those exiting the shelter gasped at the sight. As Auntie Cathy and Auntie Lilly stepped out of the shelter, Auntie Lilly was holding Tony in her arms. She let out a scream.

"No, No! Not my house!" She pushed the baby into my mum's arms and started to run forward. Other mothers gasped and ran forward to follow her, but the warden reached out his hands.

"Sorry, love, but you can't come any nearer; too dangerous!" I watched him through the fog as he tried to reassure her. Then I heard her scream at him, "That's where I live!"

She fought with the warden, but he wouldn't let her pass. She turned and stumbled towards us as we waited. She looked at Granddad, her skin ashen.

"All my things, Dad! I'd just finished the ironing and… and…" She glanced up to the sky, her breathing becoming erratic; her eyes dilating. She staggered forward and fell into Granddad's waiting arms. He carried her limp body to his house and laid her gently on the horse hair sofa.

My Auntie Cathy's house was still standing, so she went home to see the damage. Grandma busied herself and made some tea as she stared at her cracked ceiling. Auntie Lilly looked so thin and fragile as she lay there, so still. Granddad patted her face with a moist flannel and she stirred and opened her eyes. She looked so much like my dad.

"Has it all gone, Dad?" she whispered.

He stroked her forehead, "Yes, love, but you can stay here. We'll soon sort out a bed for you and the boys."

Victor and Tony were eating bread and dripping, unconcerned. Victor turned to his mum.

"Can I go and get my toy truck, Mam?"

Granddad shushed him. "Your house isn't there anymore, Victor! A bomb dropped on your house and everything has been destroyed."

Auntie Lilly moaned aloud. Victor just pulled a face.

Auntie Lilly was shaking uncontrollably as she struggled to sit up. "There's no food, clothes, bedding; all my furniture; oh, all my pictures, my photographs; all gone forever. It's all gone, Dad!" She held her head in her hands and wept uncontrollably. I sat quietly in the corner of the room and felt so angry, so useless and unhappy. My grandma put her arms around Lilly's shoulders.

"Come on, love, try and drink some tea; it'll do you good, you've had a terrible shock. You must rest."

My mum turned to Aunt Lilly. "I felt just the same when I lost my shop."

I wanted to contradict my mother. How could she know what it feels like to lose your home? But I suppose in her own way, she was trying to console my auntie, but Auntie Lilly just sat half-crouched like a frightened rabbit.

We walked home that night, grubby, dishevelled and in sombre mood. Only the Beverley Road area had been bombed; Brunswick Avenue and the surrounding streets. I was saddened and shocked by the fact that Auntie Lilly's house had been one of those hit. Even back at home when I was relaxed, drinking my cocoa before bed, my hands were still shaking. I suppose we were all in a state of shock.

At times, my mum could be quite thoughtful. She suggested that we hunt around the house and see what items could be spared for Aunt Lilly. I sorted out my books and my toy box and we ended up with two carriers full of bedding, linen, pots and pans, toys and books for my cousins.

When I wrote in my diary that night, I used up three whole pages dramatising all the events. I felt so angry at the unforgivable, wanton destruction to innocent hard-working people; why was life so cruel? After all my writing I found it hard to get to sleep that night. I couldn't wipe away the mental picture of the horror on my auntie's face.

Chapter 15
'My New Coat'

The following day, Mum and I were to meet Grandma Emmett and my Auntie Enid at Paragon Station. Mum had managed to get the Saturday off from the cinema, where she had been working since her shop was bombed. This was a special treat, because my grandma didn't come into Hull very often. It was hard for families to get together during the war years; people didn't travel far from home in case there was a sudden raid.

I waited anxiously at the ticket barrier and, as the train pulled in, I remembered the last time I had been here and how unhappy I had felt. I shivered as these uncomfortable thoughts clouded my mind, but today was a joyous day. I was excited as Grandma stepped off the train. She wore a brown gabardine coat with one large button at the neck, she had on lisle stockings and black band shoes with Cuban heels. She held a black see-through plastic shopping bag that held her purse and hanky. My auntie followed behind her, wearing a dog-tooth check box jacket, a white blouse and a black A-line skirt, her laced-up brown brogues seemed to stand out. She was tall, like my grandma and both were very thin.

"Oh, Grandma!" I savoured the moment as we embraced, my arms outstretched around her waist; I could feel her bones. Next, Auntie Enid held my shoulders aloft and gave me a wet kiss on my cheek. My grandma looked tired and pale, but those dark, lined eyes smiled with such loving tenderness. She pushed a small parcel into my hands.

"For you, dear!"

I opened it quickly; a packet of snap cards.

"Thanks, Grandma. I can play with these with my friend, Beryl."

"Later, Mary, we have to go shopping now." Mum smiled and put them safely in her bag. "I've got a club cheque for ten pounds and Grandma has given us her clothes coupons, Mary," she gestured.

As we walked away from the station, Grandma and Auntie Enid were very shocked at all the bomb damage before them. The first sight that greeted them was the great pile of rubble that had formerly been the large 'Hammonds' store. There were numerous smaller shops and other damaged buildings with the odd wall at an angle defying gravity.

There was much activity, as news vendors shouted, "Daily Mail!", road sweepers sifted through their quarry, looking for shrapnel, a crane droned on the Hammond's site and a lorry waited, as the crane heaped the debris to be taken away. Many shops were still open, but with windows boarded up after constant blasts. It never ceased to amaze me how everyone carried on as normal after such devastation. We walked towards Queen's Gardens. The fountains stood silent, not a drop of water flowing and a few bedding plants gave a little colour against the green of the grass. We sat for a little while and Grandma gave me some bread for the pigeons. They nodded their heads in agreement, as the crumbs disappeared; they were not shy birds. With my head on one side, I looked puzzled.

"Mam, I wonder where they go when the raids come?"

Mum smiled, "Oh, Mary, you do ask some questions, don't you?"

After our pause, we walked across Jameson Street, on to Saville Street and then across to Charles Street. At the beginning of this street was a very large department store. It was named 'Ansties'. To me it was like an Aladdin's cave. Mum decided to spend her club cheque here. This store sold everything. She particularly wanted to buy me a winter coat, though the choice was rather limited.

The war had affected all outfitters, deliveries and output from many factories, some of which were probably bombed or damaged, not mention much of the workforce called up to serve in the forces. Finally, Mum chose for me a fine check Harris Tweed coat in light brown. It was double breasted with two slanting side pockets and it had a secret pocket in the inside of the hem of the lining. I liked that part best of all. Mum had two pounds and five shillings left over, so she bought Dad a smart, cream check shirt and with the spare change, some hankies for Grandma.

We wandered around the shop; I looked longingly at the toys. I should feel happy I had a new coat. We sauntered along Waterloo Street, which was now quite busy and I was beginning to feel a little peckish. I studied Mackman's cake shop; everything looked very tempting. The window groaned with scones, teacakes and iced fingers, but in one corner, I spied Devonshire splits. Grandma bought some teacakes to take home and asked for the biggest of cream buns just for me - what bliss!

When we reached the pet shop, I saw no pets, only a few budgerigars twittering in small cages. We turned back towards the town centre, then walked once more down Saville Street. I could smell coffee. The aroma came from 'Field's Café'. We went inside: Mum, Grandma and Auntie Enid drank from tiny cups, while I had a glass of milk. I wanted another cake, but Mum said that it was too expensive. I felt very fussy as I sat inside the window and watched the passers-by. It was the first time I had ever been in a cafe.

By now, Grandma was looking a little tired, but she gently patted her lips with her hanky.

"Shall we call into 'Jerome's and have Mary's photograph taken, Ethel?" She always called Mum by her full name.

Mum grinned, "What a nice idea, Mam."

I sighed; I didn't like the idea of posing to be photographed.

The shop was down Whitefriargate, a short walk away. We walked in, sat down and waited.

Mum turned my chin. "Here, let's have a look at you." She fumbled in her bag and with her clean hanky, she dabbed at my face. Then, Auntie Enid fussed around me and combed my hair, preparing me for my photo call. The photographer, a slightly-built man with a line of a moustache above his lip, nodded and smiled as he ushered me into his studio.

"Now then, my dear, a little photograph for the end of the war? It will be over soon, mark my words."

I hoped he was right.

Soon Grandma had to catch her bus. I wanted to go back with her, but Mum said I had to go to school.

"I want to see Connie the goat, Mam," I pleaded.

Mum frowned. "We will go in the summer holidays, Mary."

Grandma assured me that the goat was well, but that the last time I visited, she seemed to have some tummy trouble. I quietly bent my head in shame. Grandma and Auntie hugged and kissed me goodbye and I watched as they boarded their bus. As we sat on our 62 trolley bus, I felt happy and mellow after a grand, fruitful day.

Night after night, we slept in our shelter and there were no raids. It was wonderful to feel refreshed every day after a good night's sleep. Dad still went out after tea, but came home at a reasonable hour. He remarked how pleased he felt that people were clearing areas ready for new buildings. No matter what happened, I always felt that throughout this war, the British people gave all they had. Whatever perils came along, they fought on and never gave in. The raids seemed to be forgotten, but people had to be vigilant.

My dad told me about a man who had found a hole which had developed in his road overnight. The man decided to fill in the hole with soil and rubble from his garden, thinking he was being of help to passing traffic. My dad and other men came to inspect this helpful work. Dad had an uneasy feeling about it and a bomb disposal unit was called forthwith; sure enough, there was an unexploded bomb deep under the road.

It was back to school for me, after the best summer ever. We all went back with happy hearts and lighter steps. Full days at school and I loved it! There were odd days when some loud bang would startle the class and we were told that an unexploded bomb had been found and destroyed.

These few months before Christmas passed very quickly and it was a happy time for us all, as we made cards and calendars. Beryl and I started to plan the making of our calendars in October; such was our excitement at the potential of having a normal Christmas.

This year, we spent much more time decorating our classrooms. Other years, we had had little time or energy and were too exhausted.

Away from school, we enjoyed the thrill of going to different houses to sell the calendars we had made. Everyone, to whom we spoke as we made our rounds, talked as if we had won the war, yet nothing was definite.

Christmas was a much more relaxed affair and enjoyed very much by all.

1945 started well and I was back at school after the holidays. The weather was cold and frosty, we had had little snow. It was nice to curl up in front of our warm fire. I would sit and dream as the sparks slowly made their way up the black chimney, listening to the wireless with 'Henry Halls Guest Night' or 'Itma' or 'Can I do you now, sir?' with Tommy Handley's constant jibes about Mr Hitler. We were resigned to quiet nights of uninterrupted sleep and it was wonderful. At tea time, Dad would read out from the evening edition of the Hull Daily Mail, remarking about the Nazis' demise. The news was uplifting for us all.

We were now into March, 1945. The nights were getting lighter and, if we wrapped up well, Mum would let Beryl and I play our endless 'Double Ball' in the backyard.

One night, Mum was washing me in the tin bath by the fire and Dad had gone out as usual, when we both stared at each other in disbelief. Mum handed me a towel and she rushed to the back door and listened. It was the siren.

"Good lord," she shouted, "it's a raid." Quickly, she wrapped the towel around me and we climbed into our shelter.

"Oh, I am glad we've got this shelter, Mary."

I felt stunned, as Mum rubbed me down after my hurried wash. The familiar sounds soon began: the rumble of thunder and the crackle of guns. I switched on my torch, because Mum had plunged us into darkness. Mum was just shaking her head in disbelief.

"And I thought that it had ended," she sighed.

I struggled into my pyjamas. "Mam, it's been a year without any raids!" I couldn't believe what was happening either.

"Seems, we had only had a reprieve." Mum looked at the alarm clock, it was only 8.30pm. "He's early! Maybe it will be over in a few minutes," she whispered.

I felt so shocked. I just lay there and listened to the thunderous booms and explosions and I knew that people once more were probably getting maimed and injured, or even killed. Then I thought of Dad and hoped he would be alright.

Mum told me to try and sleep. I tried to stay awake, but because I was warm and cosy, sleep took over. The next sound I heard was the whistle from our kettle and I could hear Dad's voice. I ran into the kitchen to greet him.

"Hello, little bird," he smiled. He was very dirty, but his eyes shone.

"Dad, we had a raid."

"I know, love, but it wasn't too bad," he added, "no one hurt, just lots of noise; numerous cannon shells exploding."

"I thought the raids had stopped, Dad," I said.

Dad pulled his boots off and sighed, "Well, we all did, Mary. But I don't think we will have any more."

"I hope not," Mum muttered.

Dad walked towards the front room. "I'm going to have a rest, Eth." Dad looked tired again.

I looked toward the ceiling, sighing, "I hate you, Mr Hitler, for making my Dad so tired."

I didn't have to attend school until afternoon lessons, so I sat contentedly beside the crackling fire with my drawings and, of course, I wrote about the raid in my diary.

A fortnight passed; by then we had another raid. Mum and I were fast asleep when the siren sounded. As Mum shone her torch on the clock, it was just after midnight. We huddled together and both sighed as, overhead, bursts of thunder filled the air.

We were both so sleepy that we fell into a deep slumber. I didn't know how long the raid had lasted, but Dad always had news for us. Again, he looked worn and worried as he told us that many streets down Holderness Road had been bombed, but that there was only minor damage to homes, but he was sad because there had been casualties.

The next evening, the siren disturbed our sleep once more. As I lay there, I put my hands together and prayed for the pilots to go away. Dad came home quite late the next morning. He looked dreadfully tired again. He leaned against the wooden bath top and drew hard on his Woodbine cigarette, sighing in deep dismay, as his white smoke filtered through the air.

"Not much damage, Eth, but lots of casualties. We had lots to do." He suddenly turned and banged the bath in anger with his fist.

"People are too casual, staying under the stairs; it's so foolish."

After the death and destruction he had seen, he was angry at people's complacency; twelve people had perished that night and my dad had helped to dig someone from under their stairs. As I looked at him, I felt that he was worn out, not just physically, but mentally as well. I wanted to kiss him and make everything better.

Chapter 16
'Joy'

Last night's raid was to be the last of the hostilities. My dad talked about the war coming to an end at last, but Mum shook her head, feeling doubtful. Everyone carried on as usual; we all seemed to be waiting, but for what? At school, I was making Easter cards, but our teacher was also telling the class of other festivities and celebrations regarding the end of the war. Both Mum and Dad were not sure that it could be true, but my dad seemed to read every newspaper he could lay his hands on and he started to feel more confident as the days passed by.

The Hull Daily Mail remarked about Hitler being held in loathing and abomination by everyone. Headlines: 7th May, 1945: 'German War Complete Surrender', 'There will be no escape for these Nazis.'

Dad suggested that Mum take down our blackout curtains, but she hesitated over doing so.

On May 8th, 1945, the Prime Minister, Mr Churchill, announced on the wireless: "The hostilities will officially end after midnight, tonight."

I think people were in shock. As I walked along Newland Avenue, everything looked the same. The good thing was, it would stay the same, no more destruction, no more disturbed sleep, but people still seemed quiet and subdued. That night, I played 'Double Ball' by myself, as Beryl had gone to see her grandma in Withernsea. Mum called me in for bed. Dad was still in the house, he hadn't rushed off as usual. He stood on the back doorstep and gave a heavy sigh.

"Here, Eth, look?" Mum stepped closer to him and he put his arm around her shoulder. "Mary!" he shouted.

I ran out and stood beside him, taking hold of his hand. We all peered into the night sky.

"Calm clouds and calm skies, for always," he whispered. The sun was just going down and the sky almost appeared lilac. Everything was still and no searchlights fought for a place across the great horizon.

We stared at each other, smiling.

Dad rubbed his eyes. "You know, Eth, I could sleep for a week!"

Mum said nothing, but she gave Dad a sympathetic, loving smile.

Two days later, Mum and Dad took me to the city centre on the 62 trolley bus. There was a carnival atmosphere. The bus was very full, but everyone was laughing and joking and in party mood.

We walked through Queen's Gardens and from the ornamental fountain burst a kaleidoscope of cascading colours, as water hissed in the air. Couples hugged, people sang and danced and thronged around. All the children, like me, were given flags to wave and we all cheered. Great Union Jacks bedecked the buildings that were still standing and more flags were tied, haphazardly, to bits of iron which stuck out in the air, defiant amongst the rubble.

Effigies of Hitler were being burnt, as families crowded together in a union of sheer relief. We had all suffered fear and foreboding; now we were shedding our old skin and starting anew. Few cities had suffered as much as Hull, but beneath this gaiety there would be a quiet time when we would give a thought to all the brave souls who had given their lives for us.

Everyone relaxed and let out their inhibitions. People linked arms, united in their happiness. It was as if someone had waved a magic wand and conjured up our long lost joy. Some of the gas lamps were lit for the first time in over five years. Babies were held aloft by joyful parents, toddlers sat on grown ups' shoulders and there was a frenzied feeling of great elation. We were carried along in the jollity.

Gradually, we walked home along Spring Bank and over Botanic Railway Crossings. Houses and shops were lit up as never before, all defying the dusk of the night. People waved flags as they leaned precariously from bedroom windows; they cheered and sang as we passed by, chanting and singing, 'Good old England' and 'There'll always be an England'.

We walked down Princes Avenue and finally arrived onto Newland Avenue. Then we queued at the fish shop and Dad bought us all a two penny worth bag of well-earned chips; they tasted wonderful!

At home I sat with my cup of cocoa and sighed, as my body ached with a cosy sort of tiredness. I wondered if we would ever get back to normality. This drastic change would take us all a long time to adjust to.

Dad smiled at me, "Come here, little bird."

I gently sat on his knee. He hugged me and kissed my cheek. "Wasn't it a wonderful sight, to see so many happy people, Mary?"

I nodded, feeling overwhelmed. Dad didn't look tired anymore and I felt happy.

"I'm going to write about this in my diary, Dad, I have so much to say."

"Then it's time for bed! You need your rest after such an exciting day," he laughed.

He walked into the yard and started to check the tyres on his bike and I realised I would never see his furrowed brow, heavy with lack of sleep, again. I watched Mum as she washed a few pots in the sink.

As I sipped my cocoa, I looked around and pondered upon my short life. Such a lot had happened and the war was now really at an end. We had had over five years of uncertainty, now we could be normal again, whatever that meant! I would never, ever take anything for granted.

I would never forget Aunt B, she had given me love and wisdom. I would always be grateful for that. My mother, like other mums, had fought her own private battle and she had shown me how to try harder to cope with trials in my future. My dad had given me the ability to use my imagination and to think of others along the way. This ordinary man created a power, a capacity and an energy, by helping others. He never gave up, no matter what the odds. He taught me benevolence, which I shall have for the rest of my days.

My life had been spared and in a month's time I would have lived a decade, but it seemed like a century. I had dealt with my own conflict and I had won.

We now shared a victory, but at a price. There must never be another war and I must never hate. Hate is a bad word!

This was my last entry in my diary….

About the Author

Born in Hull on the 24th June, 1935, Ethel Mary Dickinson, known as Mary to her family and friends, was an accomplished seamstress and creative writer of poetry and short stories. Mary had a creativity and passion that she applied to all aspects of her life, much of which stemmed from her early experiences, growing up during the Second World War and the inspirational people she met. Mary lived in Hull all her life and was one of two children. Mary had a family of four children and was a devoted wife, mum and grandma.

Mary spent several years writing this book and spent many long hours researching the historical facts: the once majestic Hull Museum, now nothing but a memory, the chains of the barrage balloon that had become loose from its moorings in the nearby Pearson Park, ripping away tiles, smashing windows and causing devastation in its wake, the German pilot flying in so low and firing his machine guns at people as they scrambled for cover …..some didn't make it.

Mary passed away on 29th November, 2011 and, sadly, never got to see her story published. But it is one that needs to be told, capturing a unique childhood in an extraordinary time.

Acknowledgements

When I received this book to edit, Mary Dickinson, the author, had sadly passed away. Working with her son, Philip, we began discussing this book that Mary had written. Having had some experience in authoring and publishing, I offered to help Philip and his family realise their dream; getting their Mum's book published.

I would like to take the opportunity to thank all those involved. Firstly, I would like to thank Philip and his sisters, Catherine and Christine. In what has been a difficult time in their lives, they have honoured the memory of their mum by completing the process she started. I am certain that Mary would be proud of their efforts on her behalf. I would also like to thank Kate Brennan, who graciously agreed to check my work and ensure that I was doing justice to this wonderful story.

I would also like to thank Mary herself. Even though I had not the pleasure of meeting her, I felt that I got to know a little of who she was through working on this book. Her personality and her spirit live on in the words she has written and I sincerely hope that others will get to know the little girl who became the woman her family loved so dearly.

Thank you for reading.

Graham Carmichael
(Editor)

Made in the USA
Charleston, SC
03 June 2013